WINE COUNTRY COOKING

WINE COUNTRY COOKING

Joanne Weir

TEN SPEED PRESS
Berkeley | Toronto

Ten Speed Press
PO Box 7123
Berkeley, California 94707
www.tenspeed.com

Distributed in Australia by Simon and Schuster Australia, in Canada by Ten Speed Press Canada, in New Zealand by Southern Publishers Group, in South Africa by Real Books, and in the United Kingdom and Europe by Publishers Group UK.

Cover and text design by Chloe Rawlins

Portions of this book were previously published by Time-Life Books as *Weir Cooking: Recipes from the Wine Country*.

Library of Congress Cataloging-in-Publication Data

Weir, Joanne.
  Wine country cooking / Joanne Weir.
        p. cm.
  Reprint. Originally published as: Weir cooking. Alexandria, Va. :
Time-Life Books, 1999.
  Includes index.
  Summary: "Nationally known chef and PBS television personality Joanne Weir
shares her favorite Mediterranean-inspired recipes and wine pairings from
California wine country"—Provided by publisher.
  ISBN 978-1-58008-938-8
  1. Cookery, American—California style. I. Weir, Joanne. Weir cooking.
II. Weir cooking in the wine country (Television program) III. Title.
  TX715.2.C34W45 2008
  641.59794—dc22
                            2008004515

Printed in China
First printing this edition, 2008

1 2 3 4 5 6 7 8 9 10 — 12 11 10 09 08

To Joe,

So happy I went to Wine that late April evening.
My life will never be the same.

Contents

Acknowledgments

It is truly a wonderful gift to love what you do! It makes life that much easier. To have a great team behind you also helps to lighten the load. My heartfelt thanks goes to Mariangela Sassi for her excellent advice, words of encouragement, and business savvy. I thank my lucky stars every day. A big kiss and a million thanks go to my agent and dear friend, Doe Coover, who helped make this book happen. And I would also like to thank Frances Kennedy for her hard work and perseverance. Without Frances and Doe, this book wouldn't have come to fruition. A thousand thanks to Tim McDonald, wine consultant, and Renee Nicole Kubin, sommelier at Restaurant Gary Danko, for their fantastic wine palates and intelligent wine pairings. I couldn't have better "wine pals." Thanks to Linda Read for her savvy words. Of course, my thanks to Richard Jung, whose lovely photographs grace the pages of this book. And to food stylist Allison Attenborough, thanks for your artistry and unparalleled work.

And last, but certainly not least, thanks to my editor, Lisa Westmoreland, designer Chloe Rawlins, publicist Lisa Regul, and everyone else at Ten Speed for their hard work and dedication. You have made working on this book an absolute pleasure.

The Wine Country: A Latitude and an Attitude

As strange as this may sound, my favorite places in the whole world are connected by a single straight line. It's the thirty-eighth parallel, and it runs right through all my spiritual homes: Sicily and Calabria in Italy, Murcia and Valencia in Spain, Athens in Greece, Izmir in Turkey—and, halfway around the globe—the earthly paradise so close to home, the California wine country.

As a chef, cooking teacher, and food writer, I am lucky enough to travel all over the world, but the closer I stick to that good old thirty-eighth parallel, the happier I am. And believe it or not, if I had to pick a single point on that line, I'd grab a picnic basket, jump in my car, and head north from my San Francisco home, across the Golden Gate Bridge, to "my" wine country, the nearby valleys and hillsides of Napa and Sonoma counties.

I've made that trip hundreds of times, and I've gotten to know this wine country in all its seasons: the long hot summer days, when the vines are green and heavy with grapes; the frenzied pace of the picking and crush in autumn; the quiet starkness of winter; and the magical return of spring, when the vineyards come alive with bright yellow mustard blossoms. And the more I've seen of this amazing place, the more I'm struck by how its steeply sloping hills covered with vines, intense sunlight, and vivid colors resemble the other part of the world I love so much, the Mediterranean.

Those similarities weren't lost on the early European settlers of this northern California region, who took what nature had to offer and remade it in the image of the world they had left behind, literally transplanting their roots into the rich, well-drained soil. They planted groves of olive and citrus trees, fruit and nut orchards, gardens filled with Mediterranean herbs and vegetables. And they discovered that the mild climate, with its arid summers, cool morning fog, bright and hot afternoons, and cooling Pacific breezes, was perfect for growing wine grapes.

More than 150 years later, California—along with nearby wine regions in the Pacific Northwest—produces some of the great wines of the world. The landscape first imagined by those early settlers is now lush and mature. Vineyards share the land with olive trees, green fields, and gardens that look out of southern France, Italy, or Spain, brimming with a colorful "ratatouille" of sweet tomatoes ripening on the vine; bulbs of garlic; red, green, and yellow bell peppers; squash; and eggplant. Fruit and nut trees are everywhere—Meyer lemon, fig, apple, Italian prune plum, persimmon, and walnut, and the fragrance of rosemary, basil, wild fennel, thyme, lavender, and mint fill the air.

It's no wonder this part of the world inspires cooking. More specifically, it inspires "wine country cooking"—a simple, unfussy, updated Mediterranean way of preparing and eating food that changes with the seasons and celebrates the fruits of the field, the orchard, the pasture, the river, and the sea, paired with your favorite wines. The marriage of food and wine, with all of its positive associations, is a cornerstone of wine country cooking. Nothing suits the wine country style of living and its simple, yet quenching style of cooking better than dishes that are simply cooked using the best ingredients, such as grass-fed cattle, free-range organic chicken, and freshly caught seafood. (They're also a really good excuse for a great glass of wine.) On trip after trip to places like Tuscany in Italy, La Rioja in Spain, Provence in France, and the Napa Valley of California, I've found that the dishes I love most are often the simplest—a thick juicy *bistecca alla Fiorentina* grilled over the embers in Tuscany enjoyed with Chianti, spit-roasted leg of lamb in the south of France paired with a glass of Châteauneuf-du-Pape, or wild salmon from the California Pacific coast washed down with a Pinot Noir. Nothing fancy, nothing contrived. Nothing to interfere with the essence of the matter.

Superb ingredients are a signature of wine country cooking and the farmer's market is the ultimate place to find them. On display is a bounty of what's best and most fresh, often picked that very morning. In wine country, farmer's markets are gathering spots, like town squares, for friends, families, chefs, grape growers, and vineyard owners to meet and chat as they shop for local field-ripened vegetables and tree-ripened fruit, fragrant flowers, impeccable fish, artisan breads and pastries, plus delicacies such as cheeses and olive oil. It's a year-round show: Winter brings colorful squashes, robust greens, hearty root vegetables, and wild mushrooms. In spring, the market is filled with green, as the new season brings lettuces, pea shoots, baby leeks, and green garlic. Then, the fabulous vegetables and fruits of summer, which need only the simplest preparations, so the cooking is easy. There are vine-ripened heirloom tomatoes, melons, berries, plump figs, corn-on-the-cob, sweet bell peppers, summer squash, green beans, garlic, and all kinds of fresh herbs to sprinkle over them. As the days grow shorter and the sun more scarce, the farmer's market becomes a cornucopia of earthy fall vegetables and fruits: grapes of all kinds, pumpkins, hard-shelled squashes of every color and shape, wild mushrooms, and root vegetables.

Many grape growers are also olive growers, and it's impossible to think of wine country and not think of olive oil and olives. The gnarly olive tree, with its shimmering silver-green leaves is native to the wine countries of the south of France, Italy, Greece, California, Australia, New Zealand, South America, and South Africa and shares the same land as the vine. Both grapes and olives thrive in the Mediterranean climate of dry summers and wet winters. As essential as grapes and grapevines are to winemaking, olives and olive oil are pivotal in wine country cooking. I buy bottles of extra-virgin olive oil like I do wine, each specially chosen to complement a different mood, a different dish, a different flavor. I use fruity, peppery, complex extra-virgin olive oils for dressings, pastas, and simple dishes that allow the flavor to really shine through. "Pure" olive oil (usually a blend of refined and virgin oils) is fine for frying, but mostly I stick to extra-virgin olive oil.

A word of advice when it comes to olive oil: splurge! Buy the best olive oil you can get your hands on. For olives, try a few of the specialty varieties offered at the olive bars now proliferating at well-stocked groceries and food stores. Keep tasting and experimenting. Like that first brave soul who ever tried an olive, you'll discover that one of the wine country's great treasures is right there under your nose.

Another crop commonly grown in many wine countries is garlic, which makes its way into the cuisine with delicious results. Garlic is a dominant flavor in the cuisines of the wine regions throughout the Mediterranean, and it's the same in California wine country, whose vineyards are neighbors of the garlic fields of Gilroy, the self-described "garlic capital of the world." In early spring, just as the grapevine buds are beginning to break in the vineyards, garlic sprouts from the ground, resembling a bulbous green onion. Green garlic, the immature bulb harvested later in the spring, is not nearly as assertive as mature garlic. It's perfect for dishes like soups, savory flans, soufflés, and pasta, where the flavor of garlic is meant to perfume, not overpower. During the hot months, the bulbs are mature and strongly flavored, ready to season the bright, simple foods of lazy summer days or to hang in a cool, dark place until dry for use during the fall and winter. As you can see, garlic plays an important role in the wine country kitchen at every stage of its development.

Just like garlic, cheeses and other artisanal products are produced in these regions. A new crop of farmers and cheesemakers—many based in the wine country—are discovering the beauty of farmstead and artisanal cheeses. Like winemakers and olive oil producers, they have elevated crafting cheese to an art. They've learned that similar to wine, the taste of cheese can be affected by environmental factors (*terroir*), as well as when and how a cheese is produced. Artisanal cheeses are typically handmade in small quantities using traditional methods, local ingredients, and minimal mechanization, while farmstead cheeses are made from the farmer's own milk producers (cows, sheep, goats) and crafted on site. On wine country menus, cheeses are often paired with fine wines, featured in elaborate recipes, or served as a separate course after the main course and combined with heirloom dried fruit, rustic breads, new-crop almonds and walnuts, rustic crackers, and organic chutneys.

Another facet of wine country cooking is rustic breads and pizzas. The oldest evidence of leavened bread was unearthed in Egypt, and Mediterranean-inspired cooks have loved wood-fired breads ever since! The desire for fresh, handmade whole-grain breads is within every one of us. Maybe it's the urge to return to nature, the way things once were, with the simplicity, the low-tech process of it all. There are no gas jets, no fancy equipment, no mysterious ingredients. It takes flour, water, salt, and heat to make bread that's as good as anything you can imagine. Of course, you also need the human element—hands to work the dough, eyes to watch it rise and brown, a nose to sense the moment it's done, and happy mouths to taste the baker's art. It all comes down to the human element, just like winemaking, where you need hands to pick the grapes, a nose to smell the bouquet, and a mouth to taste its goodness. The connection comes full circle when you put it all together, since fresh breads and hand-thrown pizzas pair so well with wine!

You can probably tell by now that food is a really important component of the wine country, but it's also about lifestyle—magical, simple, and pure, life in the slow lane with all the right priorities. It's taking an extra moment to really savor a great glass of wine or a lunch based on luscious fresh vegetables from your own garden or bought at your local farmer's market. It's spending the whole afternoon cooking and catching up with family and friends. It's long, leisurely al fresco dinners, filled with laughter and stories and big, bright platters of food that sparkle in the candlelight under a blanket of stars.

And, of course, as people seldom eat in wine country without drinking something, it's the love of pairing food and wine to bring out the best qualities of both. Wine is part of everyday life, not an afterthought. Wine *is* food. And in that spirit, I urge you—if you're someone who worries about which food goes with which wine—to set aside what you've read or heard about the "rules" of food-and-wine pairing. Forget about "white with chicken, red with meat." Instead, think about how all the components of a dish go together. You're braising some chicken with olives? Syrah pairs beautifully with the assertive flavor of olives. Yes, a red wine with chicken!

Here are some casual guidelines for pairing wine and food that work for me. Perhaps you've heard that salad can't be served with wine because of the acidity of the vinaigrette. Try a Sauvignon Blanc, which often makes a perfect complement to salad. Or experiment with reducing the acidity of the vinaigrette and adding a bit more oil. One of my favorite vinaigrettes, which is very wine-friendly and so very, very simple, is made by boiling a cup of wine—Riesling or Gewürztraminer works well—until it is reduced to just a couple of tablespoons and has a syrupy consistency, then whisking in some fruity olive oil and a pinch of salt. Toss it with some salad greens and slices of peach, nectarine, plum, or pitted cherries, and a few toasted almonds. Maybe throw a little fresh goat cheese on top. Serve it with the same wine you used in the vinaigrette, and you'll be pleasantly surprised.

Keep in mind that the more a wine ages in oak barrels, the more difficult it is to pair with food; oak dampens the fruitiness of wine and masks the flavor of food. I like wines with just a kiss of oak that lets the freshness of the fruit and the brightness of the flavor shine through. Also, take the weight and richness of food into account when pairing with wine. If you have a rich sauce, think rich wine!

Salty and acidic foods decrease the acid perception of wine, making it taste sweeter. Sweet food has the opposite effect—wine tastes more acidic and less sweet. Spicy foods bring out the tannins in wine, while rich, fatty foods decrease the perception of a wine's acidity and tannins. But, in the end, the important rule is this: follow your nose and your taste buds, and enjoy what tastes good to you. Drink wines that you like, eat foods that you like, and the rest will fall into place.

The same holds true for cooking. I'm always encouraging my students, my family, and my friends to experiment and try new things. Maybe it's mastering a new cooking technique. Or perhaps it's trying a new ingredient. So, go ahead. Toss a little shaved fennel into that salad. Try cooking a chicken under a brick. How about shucking some fresh fava beans when they are at their springtime best, or maybe even growing some yourself? After all, how will you know what you might be missing unless you take some chances every now and then?

Before I send you into the kitchen, here are a few key techniques you'll use over and over in wine country cooking. Turn to this page as an easy reference when you come across these instructions in the recipes.

Peeling, Seeding, and Chopping Tomatoes

Have ready a bowl of ice water. With a small paring knife, cut a cross through the skin on the bottom of the tomato. Bring a large pot of water to a boil. Add the tomatoes and boil for 30 seconds. Remove with a slotted spoon and immediately place in the ice water to cool. Remove the tomatoes from the water and, with a small knife, core the tomatoes. Remove the skins. Discard the skins and cores. Imagine the core is the North Pole and cut across the equator. Cup the tomato halves, one in each hand. Squeeze the tomatoes to remove the seeds. Chop the tomatoes.

Roasting Bell Peppers

Place the peppers directly on the gas jets of your cooktop or on an outdoor grill and char the peppers on all sides until the skins are completely black. Alternately, halve the peppers lengthwise and remove the stems, seeds, and ribs. Place the halves, cut side down, on a baking sheet. Broil until the skins are black, 6 to 10 minutes. Transfer the peppers to a paper or plastic bag, close tightly, and let cool for 10 minutes. Scrape off the skins with a knife. Cut the peppers into $^1/_4$-inch strips and then across into a $^1/_4$-inch dice.

Toasting Nuts

To toast pine nuts, pecans, walnuts, pistachios, or almonds, place them on a baking sheet in a 375°F oven for 5 to 7 minutes, until light golden and hot to the touch.

Keep things simple and focus on the goodness of the ingredients, and it will all work out. That's how we do things in the wine country. And having cooked and eaten all over the planet, I can tell you that the wine country is a state of mind. It's relaxed, refreshing, and festive, filled with lively flavors and brimming with possibilities. I hope this book gives you a taste of that happy state of mind and brings a world of delicious possibilities to your table. So grab a glass of wine, put on an apron, and join me in the kitchen!

Soups

Cannellini Bean Soup with Rosemary Olive Oil • 10

Golden Gazpacho with Garlic Croutons • 11

Oven-Roasted Beet Soup with Watercress • 12

Harvest Vegetable Soup with Pesto • 14

Asparagus Soup with Lemon Crème Fraîche • 15

Yellow Split Pea Soup with Spiced Yogurt Garnish • 16

Roasted Cauliflower Soup with Coriander • 17

Sugar Pumpkin Soup with Honey-Pecan Butter • 18

Escarole, Egg, and Pancetta Soup • 19

Roasted Corn and Crab Chowder • 20

Salmon, Leek, and Fennel Chowder with Sizzled Leeks • 22

White Bean Soup with Smoked Ham, Tomatoes, and Mint • 23

cannellini bean soup with rosemary olive oil

Perfect for a chilly evening, this soup is hearty enough to serve as a main course. All you need is a loaf of crusty sourdough bread, a garden salad, and a bottle of Chianti to make it a meal. You can prepare this soup a few days ahead, and store it in the refrigerator until needed. Then, to serve, all that's left to do is reheat it and ladle into individual bowls. Note that the dried beans must soak for four hours or overnight before using.

$1^{1}/_{2}$ cups dried white navy or cannellini beans

$^{1}/_{4}$ cup extra-virgin olive oil

1 medium-size yellow onion, finely chopped

1 carrot, finely chopped

1 celery stalk, finely chopped

2 garlic cloves, minced

$^{1}/_{2}$ teaspoon chopped fresh rosemary

9 cups chicken stock, vegetable stock, or water

1 red bell pepper, roasted (page 6)

1 yellow bell pepper, roasted (page 6)

$^{1}/_{4}$ cup imported black olives, pitted and diced

1 tablespoon chopped fresh flat-leaf parsley

1 tablespoon red wine vinegar

Salt and freshly ground black pepper

2 sprigs of fresh rosemary

Pick over the beans and discard any stones or damaged ones. Cover with cold water and soak for 4 hours or overnight. Drain and set aside.

Heat 1 tablespoon of the olive oil in a large soup pot over medium heat. Sauté the onion, carrot, and celery until soft, about 12 minutes. Add the garlic and chopped rosemary and continue to cook, stirring, for 2 minutes. Add the drained beans and stock, decrease the heat to low, and simmer slowly for 1 to $1^{1}/_{2}$ hours, until the beans are tender. Remove from the heat and let cool slightly.

Meanwhile, in a small bowl, combine the red and yellow bell peppers, olives, parsley, red wine vinegar, and 1 tablespoon of the olive oil. Season to taste with salt and pepper; reserve for the garnish. With the spine of a chef's knife, tap the herb sprigs gently to bruise the stems slightly. Warm the remaining 2 tablespoons oil with the rosemary sprigs. As soon as the oil sizzles, remove the oil-herb mixture from the heat and let cool for 1 hour. After 1 hour, strain the oil and discard the rosemary. Reserve for drizzling.

Puree one-third of the cooked and slightly cooled beans in a food processor or blender. Return the puree to the soup. Season to taste with salt and pepper.

To serve, ladle the soup into bowls and drizzle with rosemary oil. In the center of each bowl, garnish with a spoonful of the chopped peppers and olives and serve immediately.

Serves 6

TO DRINK: Sangiovese

golden gazpacho with garlic croutons

Native to Spain, where summers are blazing hot, this delicious chilled tomato-based soup refreshes like nothing else. Here at home, wherever there is the smallest patch of soil or sunny corner, you will find tomatoes growing during the summer. They get canned, frozen, squeezed, sliced, oven-dried, and stewed. For this ice-cold soup, use the ripest tomatoes picked fresh from the garden. If yellow tomatoes are unavailable, red ones work well in this dish.

4 pounds ripe yellow tomatoes, peeled, seeded, and chopped (page 6)

1 yellow or green bell pepper, seeded and coarsely chopped

1 medium-size red onion, coarsely chopped

1 large cucumber, peeled, halved, seeded, and coarsely chopped

6 tablespoons red wine vinegar

3 large garlic cloves, minced

3 tablespoons extra-virgin olive oil

1 slice coarse-textured country-style bread, crusts removed, soaked in water, and squeezed dry

Salt and freshly ground black pepper

GARNISH

2 tablespoons extra-virgin olive oil

3 garlic cloves, crushed

6 slices white bread, crusts removed and cubed

$1/4$ cup diced green bell pepper

$1/4$ cup peeled, seeded, and chopped cucumber

$1 1/2$ cups red cherry tomatoes, quartered

$1/4$ cup diced red onion

For the soup, in a bowl, mix the tomatoes, bell pepper, onion, cucumber, vinegar, garlic, olive oil, and bread. In batches, puree the soup in a blender on high speed, about 3 minutes per batch, until very smooth. Strain through a coarse strainer into a large bowl. Season with salt and pepper, place in the refrigerator, and chill for 1 hour.

For the garnish, warm the olive oil in a skillet over medium heat. Add the crushed garlic and cook, stirring constantly, until the garlic is golden brown, about 1 minute. Remove the garlic and discard. Add the bread cubes and stir to coat with olive oil. Cook slowly, stirring occasionally, until the bread cubes are golden, 10 to 12 minutes.

To serve, ladle the chilled soup into bowls and garnish with the croutons, bell pepper, cucumber, tomatoes, and red onion. Serve immediately.

Serves 6

TO DRINK: Albariño or Tempranillo

oven-roasted beet soup
with watercress

I don't think there is any vegetable more maligned than beets. I think it comes from all those recipes from the fifties saying to boil beets to within an inch of their lives and then throw the flavor out with the cooking water. My favorite way to cook beets is to roast them in the oven, which coaxes out their natural sweetness and complex, earthy flavors. You can even roast them a day ahead of when you need them. It's all about the roasting with this soup!

2^1/$_2$ pounds beets, greens removed
  and washed
2 tablespoons extra-virgin olive oil
1 cup plus 1 tablespoon water
Salt and freshly ground black pepper
1 large red onion, minced
5 cups chicken stock
1 bunch watercress, stems removed
  and leaves chopped
^{1}/$_2$ cup crème fraîche
1 teaspoon lemon juice

Preheat the oven to 375°F.

To roast the beets, place them in a shallow baking pan and drizzle with the oil and the 1 tablespoon water. Roll the beets to coat with oil. Season with salt and pepper, cover with aluminum foil, and bake until the beets are tender and can be easily pierced with a fork, 60 to 80 minutes, depending on the size of the beets. When the beets are tender, remove them from the oven and let cool. This can be done a day in advance.

In the meantime, pour the oil from the baking pan into a soup pot. Warm the oil over medium heat, add the onion, and cook, stirring occasionally, until soft, about 7 minutes.

When the beets are cool enough to handle, peel and chop them coarsely. Add the chopped beets to the onion along with the chicken stock and the 1 cup water. Increase the heat to high and bring to a boil. Decrease the heat to low and simmer for 20 minutes. Let cool for 10 minutes.

In batches, puree the soup in a blender on high speed, 3 minutes per batch, until very smooth. Strain through a fine mesh strainer into a clean soup pot. Season to taste with salt and pepper.

Reserve ^{1}/$_4$ cup of the watercress for a garnish. In the blender, puree half of the watercress with the crème fraîche until very smooth. Add the remaining watercress and pulse 2 or 3 times. Add the lemon juice and season to taste with salt and pepper.

To serve, heat the soup. Ladle the soup into bowls and swirl the watercress crème fraiche onto the top. Garnish with the reserved chopped watercress and serve immediately.

Serves 6

TO DRINK: Beaujolais or Brouilly

harvest vegetable soup with pesto

Not many places can elicit more giddy anticipation from me than when I'm in a garden full of fresh vegetables. Grab a basket and pick whatever you'd like to make a fresh vegetable soup—you can't go wrong. The best part? The heady, sweet basil pesto swirled into the soup just before serving. Be sure to pass the rest of the pesto at the table so your guests can help themselves to more. Don't forget a big basket of crusty bread! Plan enough time to soak the dried beans for at least four hours before using.

$^1/_2$ cup dried cannellini beans

6 tablespoons extra-virgin olive oil

1 small yellow onion, chopped

2 small carrots, peeled and cut into
$^1/_2$-inch dice

2 small celery stalks, cut into $^1/_2$-inch dice

2 cups peeled, seeded, and chopped
tomatoes (fresh or canned) (page 6)

4 cups chicken stock

3 cups water

$^1/_2$ cup packed fresh basil leaves,
washed and dried

1 tablespoon pine nuts, toasted (page 7)

1 garlic clove, minced

1 cup grated Parmigiano-Reggiano cheese

Salt and freshly ground black pepper

$^1/_2$ pound green beans, ends trimmed and
cut diagonally into 1-inch lengths

$^1/_4$ pound fusilli pasta

3 cups lightly packed Swiss chard leaves
(1 small bunch) cut into 1-inch pieces

Pick over the cannellini beans and discard any stones or damaged ones. Cover with cold water and soak for 4 hours or overnight. Drain the beans and place them in a large saucepan with plenty of water. Simmer over medium-low heat, uncovered, until the beans are tender, 45 to 60 minutes. Drain the beans and reserve.

Heat 2 tablespoons of the olive oil in a large soup pot over medium-low heat. Add the onion, carrots, and celery and cook, stirring occasionally, until the vegetables are tender, about 20 minutes. Add the tomatoes, stock, and water and simmer until the vegetables are tender, about 45 minutes.

In the meantime, make the pesto. Place the basil, pine nuts, garlic, the remaining 4 tablespoons olive oil, and $^1/_2$ cup of the Parmigiano in a blender or food processor. Blend at high speed until well mixed, about 1 minute. Stop and scrape down the sides periodically and continue to blend until smooth. Season with salt and pepper. Reserve.

Fifteen minutes before serving, add the cooked cannellini beans, green beans, and pasta to the stock mixture, and simmer, covered, until the pasta is completely cooked, 8 to 10 minutes. Add the Swiss chard and simmer until it wilts, about 5 minutes. Season with salt and pepper.

Ladle the soup into bowls, top with a large spoonful of pesto, sprinkle with the remaining $^1/_2$ cup Parmigiano, and serve.

Serves 6

TO DRINK: Sauvignon Blanc or Pinot Grigio

asparagus soup with lemon crème fraîche

Early harbingers of spring, along with crocuses, jonquils, and budding grapevines, are the slender green tips of asparagus poking their heads through the soil. I know that warm weather is just around the corner and that I'll soon be savoring this most elegant vegetable. A good drizzle of lemon-scented crème fraîche makes every spoonful of this springtime soup come alive in your mouth.

3 pounds asparagus, ends removed and discarded
2 tablespoons unsalted butter
1 onion, coarsely chopped
6 cups chicken stock
2 tablespoons lemon juice
Salt and freshly ground black pepper
$^1/_2$ cup crème fraîche
1 teaspoon grated lemon zest
1 to 2 tablespoons water

Slice off 1 inch of the asparagus tips. Diagonally slice the pieces into thin slivers. Reserve. Slice the remaining asparagus into $^3/_4$-inch lengths. Reserve separately.

Melt the butter in a soup pot over medium heat. Add the onion and cook, stirring occasionally, until soft, about 7 minutes. Add the $^3/_4$-inch lengths of asparagus and the chicken stock. Bring to a boil over high heat, decrease the heat to low, and simmer until the asparagus is tender, about 12 minutes. Let the soup cool for 15 min-utes. In batches, puree the soup in a blender on high speed, 3 minutes per batch, until very smooth. Strain through a fine mesh strainer into a clean soup pot. Add 1 tablespoon of the lemon juice and season with salt and pepper. Add additional water to correct the consistency if the soup is too thick.

In a bowl, mix together the crème fraîche, lemon zest, remaining 1 tablespoon of lemon juice, and salt and pepper. Add 1 to 2 tablespoons of water to thin slightly to make a pourable consistency for drizzling over the finished soup.

To serve, bring the soup to a simmer over medium heat. Add the reserved asparagus tips to the hot soup and simmer slowly until they are tender, 2 to 3 minutes. Ladle the soup into bowls. Drizzle with the lemon crème fraîche and serve immediately.

Serves 6

TO DRINK: Sauvignon Blanc

yellow split pea soup with spiced yogurt garnish

Fresh, pungent ginger, sweet carrots, and split peas make a hearty and aromatic soup inspired by Moroccan cusine. Spiced yogurt drizzled over adds freshness and depth. Serve this soup with a great red wine and thick, buttered slices of whole-grain bread.

1 1/2 cups yellow split peas (about 1 pound)

3 tablespoons unsalted butter

1 medium-size yellow onion, chopped

1 carrot, diced

2 teaspoons grated fresh ginger

7 cups chicken stock, vegetable stock, or water

Salt and freshly ground black pepper

GARNISH

1/2 cup plain yogurt

1/8 teaspoon ground turmeric

1/8 teaspoon ground cumin

1/8 teaspoon ground coriander

Salt and freshly ground black pepper

1/4 cup whole fresh cilantro leaves

Pick over the split peas and discard any debris. Rinse them well. Drain.

Melt the butter in a soup pot over medium heat. Add the onion and carrot and cook, stirring occasionally, until soft, about 10 minutes. Decrease the heat to low, add the split peas, ginger, and stock, and simmer until the split peas are completely soft, 45 to 60 minutes. Season with salt and pepper. Cool slightly. In batches, puree the soup in a blender on high speed, 3 minutes per batch, until very smooth. Thin with water or stock if needed.

To make the garnish, in a small bowl, whisk together the yogurt, turmeric, cumin, and coriander. Season with salt and pepper.

To serve, heat the soup and ladle it into bowls. Drizzle with the spiced yogurt and garnish with fresh cilantro leaves.

Serves 6

TO DRINK: Greco or Falanghina

roasted cauliflower soup with coriander

Roasting the cauliflower with coarsely ground coriander seed gives this autumn soup a wonderfully toasty flavor with lots of depth. Pureeing it in a blender at high speed produces a lovely, silken texture. Homemade croutons add crunch to the finished masterpiece. Your friends will clamor for this soup again and again.

CROUTONS

2 cups coarse-textured bread,
    torn into ³/₄-inch cubes

2 tablespoons extra-virgin olive oil

Salt

SOUP

2 medium-size heads cauliflower,
    cored and coarsely chopped

¹/₄ cup extra-virgin olive oil

Salt and freshly ground black pepper

1 tablespoon coriander seed

1 large yellow onion, diced

3 cups chicken stock

¹/₂ cup half-and-half

Preheat the oven to 350°F.

To make the croutons, place the bread cubes on a baking sheet in a single layer. Drizzle with the 2 tablespoons olive oil and sprinkle with salt. Bake in the oven, tossing occasionally, until golden and crispy, 10 to 12 minutes. Reserve.

To make the soup, place the cauliflower in a baking pan. Drizzle the cauliflower with 2 tablespoons of the olive oil, sprinkle with salt and pepper, and toss to coat lightly. Bake until tender, about 45 minutes.

Heat a small frying pan over medium-high heat. Add the coriander seed and toss constantly until they smell fragrant, about 30 seconds. Place the toasted seed in an electric coffee or spice grinder and pulverize. If you don't have an electric grinder, either use a mortar and pestle or place the seed in a towel and pound with a heavy pan or meat mallet.

Heat the remaining 2 tablespoons olive oil in a large soup pot over medium heat. Add the onion and ground coriander seed and cook, stirring occasionally, until the onion is soft, about 10 minutes. Add the cauliflower, chicken stock, and enough water just to cover the cauliflower by 1 inch. Bring to a boil over medium-high heat and simmer for 10 minutes. Remove from the heat and let cool.

In batches, puree the soup in a blender on high speed, 3 minutes per batch, until very smooth. Add the half-and-half and season with salt and pepper. If the soup is too thick, add water to correct the consistency.

To serve, heat the soup and ladle into bowls. Garnish with the croutons and serve immediately.

Serves 6

TO DRINK: Prosecco

sugar pumpkin soup with honey-pecan butter

I get nostalgic when there's a chill in the air and I watch the leaves on the grapevines as they turn from green to orange, crimson, and gold. This is the time when I most yearn for my kitchen, where I can bring forth those comforting dishes of fall and winter, like this sweet pumpkin soup. If pumpkin is unavailable, butternut, acorn, and turban squash produce equally delicious results.

1 medium-size pumpkin (about 4 pounds)

3 tablespoons unsalted butter

3 tablespoons pecans, toasted and finely chopped (page 7)

1 tablespoon honey

Salt and freshly ground black pepper

2 slices bacon, diced

1 large yellow onion, chopped

6 cups chicken stock

$^{1}/_{2}$ cup heavy cream

$^{1}/_{4}$ cup orange juice

Large pinch of freshly grated nutmeg

Whole leaves of fresh flat-leaf parsley, for garnish

Preheat the oven to 375°F.

Halve the pumpkin from top to bottom and place it, cut side down, on an oiled baking sheet. Bake until the pumpkin can be easily skewered, 45 to 60 minutes. Cool for about 20 minutes. With a spoon, remove the seeds and discard. Scrape the pulp and reserve. Discard the skin.

For the honey-pecan butter, mash 2 tablespoons of the butter with the pecans and honey in a small bowl. Season to taste with salt and pepper.

Roll the butter in plastic wrap into a 1-inch diameter log. Store in the refrigerator until well chilled and firm.

Melt the remaining 1 tablespoon of butter in a soup pot over medium heat. Add the bacon and onion and cook, stirring occasionally, until the onion is soft and the bacon is just turning golden, about 7 minutes. Add the pumpkin and stock and simmer until the pumpkin falls apart, about 30 minutes. Let cool for about 20 minutes. In batches, puree the soup in a blender on high speed, 3 minutes per batch, until very smooth. Strain through a fine mesh strainer into a clean soup pot and add the cream, orange juice, and nutmeg. Season to taste with salt and pepper. If the soup is too thick, correct the consistency with additional water or stock.

To serve, ladle the hot soup into individual bowls. Cut $^{1}/_{4}$-inch slices of the honey-pecan butter and float one in each bowl of soup. Garnish with parsley leaves and serve.

Serves 6

TO DRINK: Riesling or Viognier

escarole, egg, and pancetta soup

Also known as Italian penicillin, this soup is the cure for anything from a night of too much wine to not enough sleep (those two seem to travel together, don't they?) to being just plain under the weather. Basically, this is chicken soup gussied up with garlic, wilted escarole, and eggs swirled in at the last moment. It also features pancetta, a peppered and brined unsmoked bacon that is available in most well-stocked grocery stores and Italian markets. Don't forget to sprinkle on a good handful of grated Parmigiano-Reggiano along with a drizzle of excellent-quality extra-virgin olive oil.

3 tablespoons extra-virgin olive oil,
    plus more for drizzling (optional)

3 ounces pancetta, diced

4 garlic cloves, minced

1 head escarole, coarsely chopped

8 cups chicken stock

4 cups water

1 carrot, diced

2 celery stalks, diced

1 medium-size yellow onion, diced

3 large eggs, well beaten

Salt and freshly ground black pepper

1 tablespoon chopped fresh flat-leaf parsley,
    for garnish

$^3/_4$ cup grated pecorino or Parmigiano-
    Reggiano cheese, for garnish

Warm the 3 tablespoons olive oil in a large soup pot over medium-high heat. Add the pancetta and cook, stirring frequently, until light golden, 3 to 4 minutes. Add the garlic and cook, stirring, for 30 seconds. Immediately add the escarole and cook, stirring frequently, until soft, 3 to 5 minutes. Remove from the pan and reserve.

Add the stock and the water to the soup pot and bring to a boil over high heat. Decrease the heat to low, add the carrot, celery, and onion, and simmer for 30 minutes. Transfer the escarole mixture to the pot and simmer for 7 to 10 minutes. Add the eggs and stir vigorously for 30 seconds. Season with salt and pepper.

Serve sprinkled with parsley and grated Parmigiano cheese. Drizzle with olive oil.

Serves 6

TO DRINK: Sangiovese

roasted corn and crab chowder

We seem to wait all year for fresh corn-on-the-cob! The sweetness of fresh summer corn pairs beautifully with crab and makes a deliciously rich chowder. Pop open a chilled bottle of Chardonnay, and voilà! You can make this soup a couple of days ahead, store in the refrigerator, and heat just before serving.

6 medium-size ears fresh corn, in their husks

2 cooked Dungeness or blue crabs
   (1 to 1^1/$_2$ pounds each)

2 tablespoons unsalted butter

1 small yellow onion, chopped

4 sprigs of fresh thyme

3 bay leaves

1^1/$_2$ cups dry white wine, such as
   Sauvignon Blanc

3 cups bottled clam juice or fish stock

1^1/$_2$ cups water

^{3}/$_4$ pound potatoes, peeled and
   cut into ^{1}/$_2$-inch dice

^{1}/$_2$ cup heavy cream

Salt and freshly ground black pepper

1 tablespoon finely snipped fresh chives,
   for garnish

Heat a charcoal grill. Grill the corn 4 inches from the coals, turning occasionally, until the corn husks are black and the corn kernels are light golden when the husk is pulled back, 6 to 10 minutes. Remove the husks and silk and discard. Cut the kernels from the cob and set aside.

Clean and crack the crab, or have your fishmonger do it, and remove the meat from the body and legs. Reserve the meat in a bowl. Remove the meat from the claws and slice. Add to the bowl with the other crabmeat. Using heavy kitchen shears, cut the shells into small pieces and set aside.

In a soup pot over low heat, melt the butter. Add the onion and cook, stirring occasionally, until soft, about 10 minutes. Add the crab shells, thyme, bay leaves, wine, clam juice, and water. Bring to a boil over medium-high heat, decrease the heat to low, cover, and simmer for 20 minutes. Strain and discard the shells.

Reserve 1 cup of corn for garnish. Add the remaining corn to the crab broth and simmer until reduced by one-quarter, about 15 minutes. In batches, puree the soup in a blender on high speed, 3 minutes per batch, until very smooth. Strain through a fine mesh strainer lined with cheesecloth into a clean soup pan.

Bring a large saucepan three-quarters full of salted water to a boil over medium-high heat. Add the potatoes and cook until tender, about 10 minutes. Drain and reserve.

To the pureed soup, add the cream, reserved crabmeat, reserved corn, and the potatoes. Season to taste with salt and pepper. Heat over medium-high heat just until hot, 3 to 4 minutes. Serve immediately, garnished with chives.

Serves 6

TO DRINK: Chardonnay or rich Sauvignon Blanc

salmon, leek, and fennel chowder with sizzled leeks

Every once in a while you just have to give in and make something rich and extravagant. This soup fits the bill: a creamy and decadent pureed soup of leeks and fennel finished with poached salmon and a touch of cream. A pile of golden, crispy leeks as the finishing touch adds texture and a little drama.

3 medium-size fennel bulbs, with
    stalks and greens

4 leeks, white and 1 inch of the green parts,
    coarsely chopped

3^1/$_2$ tablespoons extra-virgin olive oil

3 cups bottled clam juice

2 cups water

1 cup canola oil

1 leek, including 1 inch of light green, cut
    into 1^1/$_2$-inch julienne, for garnish

^{1}/$_2$ cup heavy cream

Salt and freshly ground black pepper

12 ounces salmon fillet, skin and bones
    removed, cut into ^{1}/$_2$-inch pieces

Remove the green fennel tops; chop coarsely and reserve. Trim the stem ends of the fennel and discard any outside leaves that are damaged. Chop the fennel coarsely. Wash the chopped leeks and drain well.

Heat 2 tablespoons of the olive oil in a large soup pot over medium-low heat. Add the fennel and leeks and sauté until the leeks are soft, 10 to 15 minutes. Add the clam juice and the water and bring to a boil over medium-high heat. Decrease the heat to low and simmer until the fennel is soft, about 20 minutes.

Twenty minutes before serving, heat the canola oil in a skillet over high heat until rippling. Add the julienne leek and cook, stirring, until golden. Drain on paper towels.

In batches, puree the soup in a blender on high speed, 3 minutes per batch, until very smooth. Strain through a fine mesh strainer into a clean soup pot. Add the cream and season with salt and pepper. Add the salmon and simmer for 2 to 3 minutes.

To serve, warm the soup over medium heat. Ladle the soup into bowls and top each serving with a mound of crispy leeks. Serve immediately.

Serves 6

TO DRINK: Chardonnay or Pinot Gris

white bean soup with smoked ham, tomatoes, and mint

La Rioja, the wine region in northern Spain, inspired this soup. Amazingly prolific, this wine appellation produces acres and acres of tempranillo, a very full-bodied red grape. Like tempranillo, this soup is gutsy and bursting with flavor. Allow time for the beans to soak for at least four hours.

3/4 cup dried white navy or
    cannellini beans
6 parsley stems
Pinch of dried thyme
2 bay leaves
1 tablespoon extra-virgin olive oil
4 ounces thick-sliced smoked bacon,
    cut into 1/4-inch dice
1 medium-size yellow onion, chopped
3 garlic cloves, minced
2 smoked ham hocks (about 1 pound total)
1 1/2 cups peeled, seeded, and chopped
    tomatoes (fresh or canned) (page 6)
6 cups chicken stock
3 fresh mint stems, bruised with the
    back of a knife
Salt and freshly ground black pepper
5 tablespoons chopped fresh mint,
    for garnish

Pick over the white beans and discard any stones. Cover with cold water and soak for 4 hours or overnight. The next day, drain the beans and place them in a saucepan with the parsley stems, thyme, bay leaves, and enough water to cover by 2 inches. Simmer over medium-low heat until the skins just begin to crack and the beans are tender, 35 to 45 minutes; reserve.

Warm the olive oil in a soup pot over medium heat. Add the bacon and onion and cook, stirring occasionally, until the bacon has rendered some of its fat, about 5 minutes. Add the garlic and continue to cook, stirring, for 3 minutes. Add the ham hocks, tomatoes, chicken stock, and mint stems. Simmer for 1 hour.

Add the cooked beans and continue to simmer for 1 hour. Remove and discard the parsley stems, mint stems, and bay leaves. Remove the ham hocks from the pan and set aside until cool enough to handle. Remove the skin and bones from the ham hocks and cut the meat into 1/4-inch pieces. Add the ham to the soup. Season with salt and pepper. Ladle the soup into bowls and garnish with the chopped mint.

Serves 6

TO DRINK: Tempranillo

Salads

Warm Grilled Potato Salad with Olives and Parmigiano-Reggiano • 26

Tomato and Lemon Salad with Lemon-Scented Oil • 28

Grilled Salad with Peppers, Olives, and Caperberries • 29

Orange, Avocado, and Green Picholine Olive Salad • 30

Salad of Chickpeas, Olives, and Garden Herbs • 32

Asparagus, Blood Orange, and Prosciutto Salad • 33

Grilled Corn and Arugula Salad with Smoky Tomato Vinaigrette • 35

Winter White Salad with a Hint of Green • 36

Salad of Frisée, Radicchio, and Autumn Fruits • 38

Salad of Greens, Shaved Mushrooms, Asparagus, and Truffle Oil • 39

Warm Wild Mushroom, Arugula and Bruschetta Salad • 40

Fried Oyster "Caesar" • 41

Warm Squid Salad with Tangerine Oil and Olives • 42

Citrus Salad with Mint and Red Onions • 44

Mozzarella and Mâche Salad • 45

Toasted Goat Cheese Salad with Smoked Bacon • 47

Tomato and Herbed Ricotta Salata Salad • 48

Fennel, Arugula, and Radicchio Salad with Shaved Pecorino • 50

Italian Bread Salad with Tomatoes and Basil • 51

Fava Bean, Fennel, and Parsley Salad • 53

White Bean Salad with Peppers, Goat Cheese, and Mint • 54

Watercress and Beet Salad with Gorgonzola and Walnuts • 56

Height-of-Summer, Five-Tomato Salad with Gorgonzola Toasts • 57

warm grilled potato salad with olives and parmigiano-reggiano

Okay. We all love our mom's potato salad, and faithfully trot it out at every family barbecue. But are you ready for a change? Maybe something a little lighter with a twist? Try this one with potatoes hot, crisp, and golden brown from the grill tossed with olive oil, green onions, fresh oregano, briny olives, and shaved Parmigiano. I promise, nobody will miss the old-fashioned variety—not for a while, anyway!

2¼ pounds small red-skinned new potatoes

5 tablespoons extra-virgin olive oil

Salt and freshly ground black pepper

5 green onions, white and green parts, thinly sliced

2 garlic cloves, minced

2 tablespoons coarsely chopped fresh flat-leaf parsley

2 teaspoons chopped fresh oregano

½ cup imported black olives, pitted

3-ounce piece Parmigiano-Reggiano cheese

Preheat the oven to 375°F.

Wash the potatoes and place in a 13 by 9-inch baking dish. Drizzle with 1 tablespoon of the olive oil, season with salt and pepper, cover with aluminum foil, and bake until tender, 50 to 60 minutes.

Preheat an outdoor grill.

When the potatoes are tender and cool enough to handle, cut them in half. Place them in a bowl and drizzle with 2 tablespoons of the olive oil. Grill, turning occasionally, until they are hot and golden, 5 to 7 minutes. Remove from the grill and place in a large serving bowl. Add the remaining 2 tablespoons olive oil, the green onions, garlic, parsley, oregano, and olives. Season to taste with salt and pepper. Using a cheese shaver, shave long, thin pieces of Parmigiano-Reggiano cheese on top of the potatoes. Toss gently and serve immediately, while the potatoes are still warm.

Serves 6

TO DRINK: Sangiovese

tomato and lemon salad with lemon-scented oil

Here you are infusing your own olive oil with fresh lemon peel. Flavored oils are easy to make and really bring out the acidity and sweetness of fresh summer tomatoes. If you are pressed for time, you can buy lemon-flavored oil at any well-stocked grocery store.

4 large lemons

$^1/_4$ cup extra-virgin olive oil

1 small shallot, minced

Salt and freshly ground black pepper

5 large ripe, red, yellow, or orange tomatoes,
    cut into $^1/_2$-inch slices

2 cups colored cherry tomatoes, halved

Whole leaves of fresh flat-leaf parsley,
    for garnish

With a vegetable peeler, peel 2 of the lemons. Try not to remove any of the white pith. If there is white pith, scrape it off with a small paring knife. Squeeze the lemons to yield $1^1/_2$ tablespoons of juice. Reserve.

Warm the olive oil in a saucepan over medium heat. Add the lemon peel and immediately remove the oil from the heat. Stir and set aside for 1 hour.

After 1 hour, strain the oil into a small bowl and discard the lemon peel. Add the lemon juice and shallot and whisk together to make a vinaigrette. Season to taste with salt and pepper.

Slice 1 of the remaining lemons into paper-thin slices and the other into wedges. To serve, place the sliced tomatoes and lemon slices on a serving platter, alternating the colors. Top with the cherry tomatoes and season with salt and pepper. Drizzle the vinaigrette over the tomatoes, garnish with the lemon wedges and parsley leaves, and serve.

Serves 6

TO DRINK: Sauvignon Blanc

grilled salad with peppers, olives, and caperberries

In the wine country, the weather is just right for serving many dinners al fresco, and salads make a perfect choice for these relaxing outdoor meals. Olives and peppers, both Mediterranean ingredients, pair well in this make-ahead salad. I have also added caperberries, the fruit produced when capers (buds) are allowed to mature on the bush. Caperberries grow along the Mediterranean coastline and are available in most well-stocked markets. They are less briny and have a wonderful crunch to them. If they are unavailable, substitute half the amount of capers.

4 large red bell peppers, roasted (page 6)

4 large yellow bell peppers, roasted (page 6)

1/4 cup extra-virgin olive oil

1 tablespoon red wine vinegar

1 tablespoon balsamic vinegar

Salt and freshly ground black pepper

1/2 cup caperberries (about 20), drained

1/2 cup imported black olives, such as kalamata or niçoise

1 teaspoon chopped fresh oregano

1/2 cup loosely packed whole fresh basil leaves

6 slices coarse-textured country-style bread

2 garlic cloves, halved lengthwise

Cut the peppers into 1-inch-wide strips and place in a bowl.

In another bowl, whisk together 3 tablespoons of the olive oil, the red wine vinegar, and the balsamic vinegar. Season with salt and pepper. Add to the peppers and toss well. Place the peppers on a platter and sprinkle the caperberries, olives, oregano, and basil leaves on top.

Toast the bread until it is a light golden on both sides. Lightly rub 1 side of each bread slice with the cut side of the garlic. Brush lightly with the remaining 1 tablespoon olive oil. Arrange the slices of toasted garlic bread around the edges of the salad and serve immediately.

Serves 6

TO DRINK: Albariño

orange, avocado, and green picholine olive salad

Salads are not just for summer. Some of my favorites are made in the fall, winter, and spring. Late winter and early spring are the perfect time to make this colorful and flavorful salad. You'll find all kinds of citrus in the market, including sweet, burgundy red blood oranges and more acidic navel oranges. Citrus is the perfect flavor brightener for creamy avocados as well as briny green picholine olives, native to the south of France. In place of picholine olives, you can substitute meaty, sweet green Lucques olives.

2 large navel oranges

3 blood oranges

3 tablespoons orange juice

1 tablespoon balsamic vinegar

1 teaspoon honey

3 tablespoons extra-virgin olive oil

Salt and freshly ground black pepper

2 medium-size ripe avocados

3/4 cup green picholine olives, or other imported green or black olives, for garnish

4 kumquats, thinly sliced, for garnish

Fresh sprigs of chervil, for garnish (optional)

Grate enough zest from 1 of the navel oranges to measure 1 teaspoon. Set aside in a small bowl. Using a sharp knife, cut off the tops and bottoms of the navel and blood oranges to reveal the flesh. Cut off all of the peel so that no white pith remains. Cut the oranges crosswise into 1/4-inch slices. Set aside.

In the bowl containing the orange zest, whisk together the orange juice, balsamic vinegar, honey, and olive oil to make a vinaigrette. Season to taste with salt and pepper.

When you are ready to assemble and serve the salad, cut the avocados in half from top to bottom. With a sharp knife blade, tap the avocado pit so that the blade lodges in the pit. Twist the knife slightly to remove the pit. Discard. With a large spoon, remove the flesh of the avocado in 1 piece. Cut each avocado half into 8 slices.

Place the orange slices on a serving plate, alternating with slices of avocado. Drizzle the vinaigrette over the oranges and avocado. Garnish with the olives, kumquats, and chervil and serve immediately.

Serves 6

TO DRINK: Sauvignon Blanc

salad of chickpeas, olives, and garden herbs

Toss chickpeas (also called garbanzo beans) with cured green and black olives, olive oil, garlic, and all kinds of herbs from your garden in this salad inspired by the sunny south of France. Serve with grilled fresh tuna steaks or skewers of chicken. The chickpeas can be cooked a day or so in advance, or, if you're in a pinch, use canned. If you're cooking the chickpeas yourself, add the vinegar and oil while they are still warm so they will absorb their flavor.

1 cup dried chickpeas

$1/3$ cup red wine vinegar

$1/3$ cup extra-virgin olive oil

4 garlic cloves, minced

Salt and freshly ground black pepper

2 tablespoons chopped fresh basil

2 tablespoons chopped fresh flat-leaf parsley

1 tablespoon chopped fresh mint

2 teaspoons chopped fresh oregano

1 teaspoon chopped fresh thyme

$1/2$ teaspoon chopped fresh rosemary

$1/3$ cup imported black olives (such as niçoise or kalamata), pitted and coarsely chopped

$1/3$ cup imported green olives (such as picholine), pitted and coarsely chopped

4 green onions, white and green parts, thinly sliced

Sprigs of herbs, for garnish

Pick over the chickpeas and discard any stones or damaged ones. Cover with cold water and soak for 4 hours or overnight.

Place the chickpeas in a saucepan with enough water to cover by 2 inches. Simmer, uncovered, over medium-low heat until the skins begin to crack and the peas are tender, 50 to 60 minutes. Drain.

In a large bowl, whisk together the vinegar, olive oil, and garlic. Season to taste with salt and pepper. Add the chickpeas and let cool.

Add the chopped basil, parsley, mint, oregano, thyme, rosemary, olives, and green onions, and toss well. Season with additional salt and pepper, if needed. Place in a serving bowl, garnish with the herb sprigs, and serve.

Serves 6

TO DRINK: Provençal rosé

asparagus, blood orange, and prosciutto salad

Just as the buds are starting to break in the vineyard, asparagus and blood oranges are everywhere in the market. In my estimation, these are the true blessings of spring! Add a few thin slices of salty prosciutto and a blood-orange vinaigrette, and you have a simple, elegant, and, most important, tasty springtime salad. If you can't find blood oranges, navel oranges work just fine.

4 blood oranges

1/4 cup blood orange juice

2 tablespoons white wine vinegar

1/4 cup extra-virgin olive oil

Salt and freshly ground black pepper

2 pounds large asparagus spears, ends snapped off

12 thin slices prosciutto, each halved lengthwise

Grate enough zest from 1 of the blood oranges to measure 1 teaspoon. Set aside in a small bowl. Using a sharp knife, cut off the tops and bottoms of the oranges to reveal the flesh. Cut off all of the peel so that no white pith remains. Cut the oranges into sections, slicing between the membranes. Discard any seeds. Set aside in a separate bowl.

In the bowl containing the orange zest, whisk together the orange juice, vinegar, and olive oil to make a vinaigrette. Season to taste with salt and pepper.

Bring a large, shallow pan of salted water to a boil over medium-high heat. Add the asparagus and cook until just tender, 4 to 6 minutes. Remove from the water. Place in a single layer on a serving platter and cool in the refrigerator.

When the asparagus is cool, scatter the orange sections over the spears. Drizzle with the vinaigrette. Curl the prosciutto strips like ribbons, place on the salad, and serve.

Serves 6

TO DRINK: Sauvignon Blanc

grilled corn and arugula salad with smoky tomato vinaigrette

If there's anything that's literally short and sweet, it's corn season. So when sweet summer corn is available, I eat it almost every day! This salad gets its smokiness from the roasted corn, tomatoes, and bell peppers. Paired with peppery arugula and salty Parmigiano and olives, this is a delicious combination inspired by my dear friend and amazing chef, Gary Danko.

3 ears fresh corn, in their husks

2 red bell peppers

1 tomato, diced

$1/2$ garlic clove, chopped

1 tablespoon red wine vinegar

$1/4$ cup extra-virgin olive oil

Salt and freshly ground black pepper

3 bunches arugula (about 8 cups), stems removed

$3/4$ cup imported black or green olives, for garnish

$1^1/2$ cups red and yellow cherry tomatoes, halved, for garnish

3-ounce piece Parmigiano-Reggiano cheese

Prepare a charcoal grill.

Grill the corn and peppers 4 inches from the coals, turning occasionally, until the skins of the peppers are black, the corn husks are black, and the corn kernels are light golden when the husk is pulled back, 6 to 10 minutes. Remove from the grill. Transfer the peppers to a paper or plastic bag, close tightly, and let cool for 10 minutes. Let the corn cool.

Remove the corn husks and silk. Cut the kernels from the cob and set aside. Scrape the skin from the peppers with a knife. Reserve the skinned peppers separately from the corn.

In a blender, puree the peppers, tomato, garlic, vinegar, and olive oil to make a vinaigrette. Season with salt and pepper, strain through a fine mesh strainer, and reserve.

On individual serving plates, divide the vinaigrette evenly among the plates. In a large bowl, toss together the corn and arugula and distribute onto the plates. Garnish with the olives and cherry tomatoes. Shave the Parmigiano over the top. Serve immediately.

Serves 6

TO DRINK: Arneis or Fumé Blanc

winter white salad with a hint of green

During the cold months, a great wine country smell is the smoky, earthy aroma of a fire made with vine trimmings. This is when I love to head into the kitchen and get creative. In the dead of winter, a crisp salad is always welcome on the table. No tomatoes? So what? Try this salad. You'll love the sweet and tart flavors.

1 small head escarole, torn into
$1^1/_2$-inch pieces

2 heads Belgian endive, leaves separated

2 celery stalks, cut on a sharp diagonal
into thin slices

$1^1/_2$ tablespoons white wine vinegar

$^1/_4$ cup extra-virgin olive oil

Salt and freshly ground black pepper

1 Granny Smith or Pippin apple, halved,
cored, and thinly sliced

$^1/_2$ cup pecans, toasted (page 7)

$^1/_3$ cup shaved Parmigiano-Reggiano cheese

In a bowl, toss together the escarole, endive, and celery. Place in the refrigerator.

In a small bowl, whisk together the vinegar and olive oil to make a vinaigrette. Season to taste with salt and pepper.

To serve, toss the escarole mixture with the vinaigrette, apple slices, pecans, and Parmigiano. Place in a salad bowl and serve immediately.

Serves 6

TO DRINK: Sauvignon Blanc or Pinot Blanc

salad of frisée, radicchio, and autumn fruits

Some people say that wine and salad don't go together because the acids compete. This recipe uses a trick, mentioned in the introduction, that really works to solve the problem: Pour a little Riesling or Gewürztraminer wine into a saucepan and reduce it until it's syrupy. Use that wine syrup in place of some of the vinegar in your salad dressing. Make sure you serve the same wine to drink. The flavors will match perfectly, as they do here.

$^1/_2$ cup dry Riesling or Gewürztraminer

1 tablespoon sherry vinegar

3 tablespoons extra-virgin olive oil

Salt and freshly ground black pepper

2 large bunches frisée, ends trimmed

1 small head radicchio, torn into
    2-inch pieces

1 Fuyu persimmon, cut into thin slices

1 red Bartlett pear, halved, cored, and
    cut into thin slices

6 figs, halved

1 small pomegranate, peeled, with seeds
    removed and separated, for garnish

$^1/_2$ cup walnut halves, toasted (page 7),
    for garnish

In a small saucepan over high heat, reduce the wine until 1 to 2 tablespoons remain. Let cool. In a small bowl, whisk together the vinegar, reduced wine, and olive oil to make a vinaigrette. Season to taste with salt and pepper.

Place the frisée, radicchio, persimmon slices, pear slices, and figs in a bowl. Add the vinaigrette and gently toss together. Place on individual salad plates. Garnish with pomegranate seeds and walnut halves and serve immediately.

Serves 6

TO DRINK: Riesling or Gewürztraminer

salad of greens, shaved mushrooms, asparagus, and truffle oil

For years when I cooked at Chez Panisse, I made a salad similar to this one that was a favorite there. The flavors are very earthy from the mushrooms and truffle oil. If fresh, unblemished chanterelles are unavailable, use button or other cultivated mushrooms.

12 medium-size chanterelles

12 medium-size tender asparagus stalks, ends trimmed

1 tablespoon pure white truffle oil

$1/4$ cup extra-virgin olive oil

$2^1/2$ tablespoons champagne vinegar

1 small shallot, minced

Salt and freshly ground black pepper

8 cups fresh mixed baby salad greens

With a cheese shaver or mandoline, shave the mushrooms into paper-thin slices. With a knife, cut the asparagus on a diagonal into paper-thin slices. Set both aside in a bowl.

In a small bowl, whisk together the truffle oil, olive oil, champagne vinegar, and shallot. Season to taste with salt and pepper.

To serve, place the salad greens, mushrooms, and asparagus in a large bowl. Add the vinaigrette and toss together. Place on serving plates, mounding the salad in the middle of each plate. Serve immediately.

Serves 6

TO DRINK: Arneis

warm wild mushroom, arugula, and bruschetta salad

Imagine a garlicky crostini smeared with virgin olive oil topped with arugula, warm wild mushrooms, and a few shavings of Parmigiano-Reggiano. Is it a salad? Is it a crostini? Who cares? It's yummy!

5 tablespoons extra-virgin olive oil,
    plus more for drizzling

1 tablespoon lemon juice

1 teaspoon grated lemon zest

1 small shallot, minced

Salt and freshly ground black pepper

1¹/₂ pounds fresh porcini mushrooms,
    trimmed, cleaned, and halved

6 slices coarse-textured Tuscan bread

2 garlic cloves

6 cups arugula

6-ounce piece Parmigiano-Reggiano cheese

In a bowl, whisk together 4 tablespoons of the olive oil, the lemon juice, lemon zest, and shallot. Season to taste with salt and pepper. Reserve.

Heat a large skillet over high heat. Add the remaining 1 tablespoon olive oil to the pan. Add the mushrooms and cook, stirring, until golden brown and softened, 8 to 10 minutes. Season with salt and pepper. Remove from the heat.

Toast or grill the bread. Rub the toasted bread with garlic and sprinkle with salt.

In a bowl, toss together the arugula and vinaigrette. Place one piece of bread on each plate. Drizzle with olive oil and sprinkle with salt. Divide the arugula among the plates and place on the top of the bread. Top with the mushrooms. Immediately shave the Parmigiano onto the top and serve.

Serves 6

TO DRINK: Pinot Gris or Pinot Noir

fried oyster "caesar"

Every once in a while I need an oyster fix, and briny fresh oysters on the half shell are the only thing that will do the trick. But for some, eating raw oysters is an acquired taste. Well, try frying them instead! I came up with this idea as I was driving back to San Francisco from the coast with a case of oysters in the trunk. I was craving Caesar salad. I couldn't get my mind off the oysters, though. I got home and put the two together. The crunchy golden fried oysters with the cool crisp greens tossed in the rich, silky, dressing is simply delicious.

18 fresh oysters, in the shell
1/2 cup all-purpose flour
2 large eggs, plus 1 egg yolk
2 tablespoons water
1 cup dry bread crumbs
Salt and freshly ground black pepper
Oil (such as peanut, corn, or olive oil),
    for deep-frying
1 garlic clove, minced
1 teaspoon Dijon mustard
2 1/2 tablespoons lemon juice
2 anchovy fillets, boned, soaked in cold
    water for 10 minutes, patted dry,
    and mashed
1/3 cup extra-virgin olive oil
4 small hearts of romaine, leaves separated
1/2 cup grated Parmigiano-Reggiano cheese

Shuck the oysters and reserve them separately from the oyster liquor. Discard the shells.

Place the flour in a bowl. Place the whole eggs in another bowl and whisk in the 2 tablespoons water. Place the bread crumbs in a third bowl. Season the flour and bread crumbs with salt and pepper. Dredge the oysters in the flour first and tap off the excess. Next dip them into the egg mixture, and then into the bread crumbs. Reserve and set aside.

In a small saucepan, heat 1 inch of oil to 375°F.

For the dressing, whisk together the reserved oyster liquor, the garlic, mustard, lemon juice, mashed anchovies, and egg yolk in a bowl until well blended. Add the 1/3 cup olive oil in a slow, steady stream and whisk until smooth. Season to taste with salt and pepper.

Fry the oysters, a few at a time, in the hot oil until golden, about 1 minute. Remove with a slotted spoon and drain on paper towels.

To serve, place the lettuce in a large bowl and toss with the dressing until the leaves are coated. Add half of the Parmigiano and toss again. Place on serving plates, top each serving with 3 fried oysters, and sprinkle with the remaining Parmigiano. Serve immediately.

Serves 6

TO DRINK: Rosé Champagne

warm squid salad with tangerine oil and olives

Usually salads are crispy and cool, but this one is all about warmth. I love warm salads, especially this one with warm, tender squid spiked with zesty tangerines and salty olives. One word of caution: don't overcook the squid or you'll end up with very flavorful rubber bands. If you cook them for just seconds, they will be so tender they'll melt in your mouth.

5 tangerines

$1/4$ cup extra-virgin olive oil

$1^1/4$ pounds squid

3 garlic cloves, minced

8 ounces small red and yellow cherry tomatoes

3 tablespoons chopped fresh flat-leaf parsley

$3/4$ cup imported black olives

1 tablespoon lemon juice

Salt and freshly ground black pepper

Remove the peel from the tangerines with a vegetable peeler. Warm the olive oil in a saucepan over medium heat. Add the tangerine peel and immediately remove the oil from the heat. Stir together. Let sit for 1 hour, then strain and reserve the peel. Thinly slice enough tangerine peel to make 2 tablespoons of sliced peel and reserve. Squeeze 1 tablespoon of tangerine juice and reserve.

Separate the head and tentacles from the body of the squid. Cut the head from the tentacles and discard the head. Remove the clear quill bone from inside the body of the squid. With a knife, scrape away the skin, cleaning out the inside of the body at the same time. Cut the body into $1/2$-inch rings. Wash the body and tentacles well until the water runs clear.

In a large skillet over high heat, warm the tangerine oil. Add the garlic and cook just until soft, a few seconds. Add the squid and cook, stirring, until the squid turn from opaque to white and the rings are slightly firm, 1 to $1^1/2$ minutes. Remove the squid from the pan with a slotted spoon and reserve in a bowl. Increase the heat to high and reduce by half any liquid that has accumulated in the pan. Add the tomatoes and continue to cook for 30 seconds. Remove from the heat, add the parsley, olives, reserved tangerine juice, and lemon juice. Add the squid and toss together. Season to taste with salt and pepper. Place on a platter and serve immediately, garnished with the reserved tangerine peel.

Serves 6

TO DRINK: Sauvignon Blanc

citrus salad with mint and red onions

I could eat a salad every day of my life. I love the freshness and endless variations that ensure you never have to eat the same salad twice. But you will want to eat this one over and over again. Using a variety of citrus and then tempering their acidity with honey brings out the sweet and sour flavors all at the same time. Throw some mint and red onions into the mix for a burst of color and added flavor.

2 grapefruit

2 navel oranges

2 blood oranges

1/2 small red onion, cut into thin rings

1/4 cup extra-virgin olive oil

2 tablespoons orange juice

1 tablespoon white wine vinegar

2 teaspoons honey

Salt and freshly ground black pepper

2 tablespoons chopped fresh mint,
    plus mint sprigs, for garnish

Lime wedges, for garnish

Grate enough zest from the grapefruit to make 1 teaspoon zest and enough from the oranges to make 2 teaspoons zest.

In the meantime, using a sharp knife, cut off the tops and bottoms of the grapefruit, navel oranges, and blood oranges to reveal the colored flesh. For each fruit, place it on a work surface, cut side down. Using a small, sharp knife, cut off the peel and white pith from top to bottom. Flip the fruit so it rests on the other cut side and remove any white pith. Cut the grapefruit, navel oranges, and blood oranges into 1/4-inch slices, removing the seeds. Place the citrus slices on a serving platter, alternating the colors. Sprinkle over the onion rings. Set aside.

In a bowl, whisk together the grapefruit and orange zests. Add the olive oil, orange juice, white wine vinegar, and honey and whisk together to make a vinaigrette. Season with salt and pepper. Drizzle the vinaigrette onto the citrus. Sprinkle with the chopped mint, then garnish with the lime wedges and mint sprigs, and serve.

Serves 6

TO DRINK: Chenin Blanc

mozzarella and mâche salad

Insalata Caprese, the ubiquitous tomato, cheese, and basil salad, is known and loved the world over. Yes, I love it, too, but when there aren't any good tomatoes to be had, I make it with spring vegetables and herbs. The flavor combination is absolutely fantastic, and it's a nice change.

1¹/₂ pounds fava beans, in the pod

2 cups water, salted

¹/₂ pound asparagus, trimmed and cut into 1-inch lengths

1 cup shelled fresh English peas

12 ounces buffalo mozzarella cheese

1 tablespoon chopped fresh mint

2 teaspoons chopped fresh savory (optional)

1 teaspoon chopped fresh oregano

¹/₄ cup extra-virgin olive oil

Salt and freshly ground black pepper

2 cups mâche or other young, tender greens

Remove the fava beans from their pods and discard the pods. Bring a pot of water to a boil over high heat, add the fava beans, and boil for 30 seconds. Drain, cool, and peel off the outer bright green shells. Discard the shells and reserve the fava beans.

Bring the 2 cups salted water to a boil in a large saucepan over high heat. Add the asparagus and boil until bright green and almost tender, 3 to 5 minutes. Remove with a slotted spoon and reserve with the fava beans. Add the peas to the boiling water, decrease the heat to low, and simmer for 15 seconds. Drain and add to the asparagus and fava beans.

To serve, thinly slice the mozzarella and arrange on a platter. Arrange the fava beans, asparagus, and peas on the platter. Sprinkle the mint, savory, and oregano onto the mozzarella and vegetables. Drizzle with olive oil and lightly season with salt and pepper. Sprinkle the mâche over all.

Serves 6

TO DRINK: Prosecco or Malvasia

toasted goat cheese salad with smoked bacon

Food doesn't get much better than this salad of tangy, oozing, goat cheese, hot from the oven, surrounded by cool salad greens and crispy smoked bacon scattered around the edges. Pair it with a cool glass of Sauvignon Blanc and you've got perfection. The goat cheese must marinate for several hours, but is best when marinated for at least a few days before using. The herb oil can be reused.

3 small rounds fresh goat cheese
    (about 5 ounces each)
$1/2$ cup extra-virgin olive oil
8 sprigs of fresh thyme
8 sprigs of fresh oregano
2 sprigs of fresh rosemary
4 ounces smoked bacon, cut into
    $1/2$-inch dice
4 thick slices coarse-textured country-
    style bread, torn into $1/2$-inch cubes
$1/2$ teaspoon Dijon mustard
1 garlic clove, minced
$1^1/2$ tablespoons red wine vinegar
Salt and freshly ground black pepper
$1^1/2$ cups fine, dry bread crumbs
8 cups mixed baby salad greens

Cut each goat cheese round in half horizontally to make 6 discs total.

Warm 5 tablespoons of the olive oil in a saucepan over low heat. With the back of your chef's knife, tap the thyme, oregano, and rosemary sprigs to bruise the stems slightly. Add the herbs to the oil and remove the oil from the heat. Let the oil cool. Pour the oil over the goat cheese rounds, coating all sides with the oil. Let marinate for at least 2 hours, or up to 2 weeks in the refrigerator.

Preheat the oven to 325°F.

Combine the bacon and bread cubes and place on a baking sheet. Bake, tossing occasionally, until the bread and bacon are light golden, about 12 minutes. Remove from the oven and set aside. Increase the heat to 400°F.

In a small bowl, whisk together the remaining 3 tablespoons olive oil, mustard, garlic, and red wine vinegar to make a vinaigrette. Season with salt and pepper.

Season the bread crumbs with salt and pepper. Remove the goat cheese rounds from the oil and coat with bread crumbs. Place on a baking sheet and bake until the cheese is warm in the center and bubbling around the edges, 4 to 6 minutes.

Toss the vinaigrette with the greens. Arrange some greens on each salad plate and place 1 cheese round in the center. Surround the cheese with croutons and bacon and serve immediately.

Serves 6

TO DRINK: Fumé Blanc or Sauvignon Blanc

tomato and herbed ricotta salata salad

Forty million Americans grow tomatoes, a true testament that picking and eating homegrown tomatoes, warm from the summer sun, is pure joy. The quickest way to enjoy summer tomatoes—short of biting right into one—is to make them into a salad. Paired with salty ricotta salata and lots of summer herbs, this is summer sunshine on a plate.

1/2 pound ricotta salata

2 tablespoons chopped fresh basil

2 tablespoons chopped fresh chives

1 tablespoon chopped fresh mint

1 teaspoon chopped fresh oregano

1 teaspoon chopped fresh thyme

5 large ripe tomatoes, cut into 1/4-inch slices

1/2 pound assorted cherry tomatoes
(red, orange, yellow plum, green),
halved

Salt and freshly ground black pepper

1/4 cup extra-virgin olive oil

3 tablespoons balsamic vinegar

Sprigs of fresh basil, mint, oregano, and
thyme, for garnish

Crumble the ricotta salata into a bowl. Add the chopped basil, chives, mint, oregano, and thyme and mix together until all of the herbs stick to the crumbled cheese. Set aside.

Place the sliced tomatoes on a serving platter, overlapping slightly. Scatter the cherry tomatoes on top. Season with salt.

In a small bowl, whisk together the olive oil and vinegar. Season to taste with salt and pepper. Drizzle the vinaigrette onto the tomatoes and let sit for 10 minutes.

To serve, scatter the herbed cheese over the tomatoes and garnish with the basil, mint, oregano, and thyme sprigs. Serve immediately.

Serves 6

TO DRINK: Sauvignon Blanc or Pinot Gris

fennel, arugula, and radicchio salad with shaved pecorino

Combine fennel with its licorice flavor, peppery arugula, bitter radicchio, and salty pecorino to make a salad that is both flavorful and very colorful. Serve as is or with strips of grilled chicken for a delicious, balanced meal.

2 medium-size fennel bulbs, trimmed

1 small head radicchio, leaves separated
    and torn into 2-inch pieces

2 bunches arugula, stemmed

12 small radishes, thinly sliced

$^1/_4$ cup extra-virgin olive oil

2 tablespoons white wine vinegar

1 shallot, minced

1 garlic clove, minced

Salt and freshly ground black pepper

3-ounce piece pecorino cheese,
    shaved into thin slices

1 bunch baby radishes with fresh,
    bright green leaves, for garnish

With a sharp knife, a mandoline, or an electric meat slicer, shave the fennel into paper-thin slices. Place in a large bowl with the radicchio, arugula, and radishes.

In a small bowl, whisk together the olive oil, vinegar, shallot, and garlic to make a vinaigrette. Season with salt and pepper.

To serve, toss the vinaigrette with the fennel, radicchio, arugula, and radishes. Place on a platter and scatter with the shaved pecorino. Garnish with the baby radishes and serve immediately.

Serves 6

TO DRINK: Pinot Grigio

italian bread salad with tomatoes and basil

Imagine a sandwich made with the sweetest tomatoes and freshest basil from the garden. Now, tear up the bread, and toss it with the tomatoes, basil, crisp cucumbers, red onions, and a red wine vinaigrette. What you have is panzanella, a summertime staple from Tuscany. It's become summer staple at my house, too.

$1/_2$ pound coarse-textured country-style
    bread, 3 to 4 days old

$1/_2$ cup water

1 medium-size hothouse cucumber, peeled,
    seeded, and cut into $1/_2$-inch dice

Salt and freshly ground black pepper

5 medium-size ripe tomatoes ($1^1/_2$ to
    2 pounds), seeded and diced

1 medium-size red onion, diced

$1/_2$ cup fresh basil leaves

5 tablespoons red wine vinegar

2 garlic cloves, minced

$1/_3$ cup extra-virgin olive oil

Slice the bread into 1-inch slices. Sprinkle the slices with the water and let sit for 2 minutes. Carefully squeeze the bread until dry. Tear the bread into coarse 1-inch shapes and let rest on paper towels for about 20 minutes.

In the meantime, place the cucumber on another few sheets of paper towels. Sprinkle with salt and let rest for 20 minutes. Place in a colander and rinse with cold water. Dry on paper towels.

In a bowl, combine the cucumber, tomatoes, and onion. Tear the basil into $1/_2$-inch pieces and add to the vegetables. Add the bread and toss carefully.

In a small bowl, whisk together the vinegar, garlic, and olive oil to make a vinaigrette. Season with salt and pepper. Carefully toss with the vegetables and bread and set aside for 20 minutes. Place on a platter and serve.

Serves 6

TO DRINK: Vernaccia

fava bean, fennel, and parsley salad

I remember teaching a class in the little town of Strada in Chianti, Tuscany, a few years ago, and we bought a case of fava beans to make this salad. Favas must first be removed from their pods, then peeled. Peeling fava beans can be a bit of work, so I gathered several of the students around a big table, gave them each a glass of wine, and in no time they were done. They all agreed the results were worth the effort when they tasted the fresh flavors of this salad.

4 pounds fresh fava beans, in the pods

Salt and freshly ground black pepper

2 medium-size fennel bulbs, trimmed

$1/4$ cup extra-virgin olive oil

2 tablespoons lemon juice

1 garlic clove, minced

2 large bunches flat-leaf parsley, leaves picked and stems discarded

Remove the fava beans from their pods and discard the pods. Bring a pot of water to a boil over high heat, add the fava beans, and boil for 30 seconds. Drain, cool, and peel off the outer bright green shells. Season with salt and pepper and reserve.

With a sharp knife or mandoline, slice the fennel into paper-thin slices and reserve.

In a small bowl, whisk together the olive oil, lemon juice, and garlic to make a vinaigrette. Season to taste with salt and pepper.

In a bowl, toss together the fava beans, fennel, parsley leaves, and vinaigrette. Place on a platter and serve immediately.

Serves 6

TO DRINK: Vernaccia

white bean salad with peppers, goat cheese, and mint

This could easily qualify as a meal in itself. A loaf of bread, a bottle of wine, a picnic blanket, and some sunshine, and you have everything you need for a summer lunch in the vineyards. Note that the dried beans must soak for at least four hours before using.

1 cup dried white beans

6 tablespoons extra-virgin olive oil

5 tablespoons red wine vinegar,
plus more if needed

Salt and freshly ground pepper

1 red bell pepper, cored, seeded, and
cut into $^1/_4$-inch dice

1 green bell pepper, cored, seeded,
and cut into $^1/_4$-inch dice

1 yellow bell pepper, cored, seeded, and
cut into $^1/_4$-inch dice

1 small red onion, cut into $^1/_4$-inch dice

1 garlic clove, minced

5 ounces fresh goat cheese, for topping

$^1/_4$ cup fresh mint leaves, cut into thin strips,
for garnish

Pick over the beans and discard any stones or damaged ones. Cover with plenty of cold water and let soak for 4 hours or overnight. Place the beans in a saucepan with plenty of water to cover and bring to a boil over high heat. Decrease the heat to low and simmer until the skins just begin to crack and the beans are tender, 30 to 40 minutes. Drain the beans.

In the meantime, in a small bowl, whisk together the olive oil and vinegar to make a vinaigrette. Season to taste with salt and pepper. Add to the warm beans and let sit until the beans cool.

When the beans have cooled, add the diced peppers, onion, and garlic and mix well. Season with salt and pepper and additional vinegar, if needed.

To serve, place the beans in a serving bowl and crumble the cheese over the top. Garnish with the mint and serve.

Serves 6

TO DRINK: Sauvignon Blanc

watercress and beet salad with gorgonzola and walnuts

Gorgonzola is one of Italy's most prized cheeses and, I have to admit, one of my own personal favorites. Combine it with the sweetness of roasted beets and toasted walnuts to make this winter salad. The earthy taste of the beets with the creamy, sharp Gorgonzola and crunchy walnuts makes this gorgeous salad perform a symphony of flavors and textures in each mouthful.

2 pounds medium-size beets
  (red or gold), washed

$1/4$ cup extra-virgin olive oil

1 tablespoon water

Salt and freshly ground black pepper

$2^1/2$ tablespoons red wine vinegar

1 small head radicchio, torn into 2-inch pieces

3 ounces Gorgonzola cheese, crumbled

$1/2$ cup walnut halves, toasted (page 7)

$1^1/2$ cups loosely packed watercress,
  stems trimmed, for garnish

Preheat the oven to 375°F.

Place the beets in a shallow baking pan and drizzle with the oil and water. Roll the beets to coat with the oil. Season with salt and pepper, cover with aluminum foil, and bake until the beets are tender and can be easily pierced with a fork, 60 to 80 minutes, depending on the size of the beets. When the beets are tender, remove from the oven and let cool. Pour the oil from the bottom of the pan into a small bowl and reserve. When the beets are cool enough to handle, peel the beets and cut them into wedges.

In the meantime, whisk together the red wine vinegar and the reserved oil. Season to taste with salt and pepper. In a bowl, combine the beets and radicchio and toss with all but 1 tablespoon of the vinaigrette. Place the beets on a serving platter. Scatter the Gorgonzola and walnuts over the top. Toss the remaining 1 tablespoon of the vinaigrette with the watercress. Season with salt and pepper. Top the beets with the watercress and serve immediately.

Serves 6

TO DRINK: Pinot Grigio

height-of-summer, five-tomato salad with gorgonzola toasts

When I was a kid, I remember going to the grocery store and seeing four hard, pink tomatoes all lined up and packed in a plastic basket, then covered with cellophane. As the saying goes, we've come a long way, baby! At the height of summer, freshly picked vine-ripened tomatoes from the garden or rainbow-hued heirloom tomatoes from the local farmer's market are easy to find and a deliciously far cry from those hard, pink tomatoes of my youth. This is the time you want to gather as many of these sweet beauties and create an entire salad around them.

3 tablespoons pine nuts

2 tablespoons unsalted butter,
    at room temperature

3 ounces Gorgonzola cheese,
    at room temperature

3 tablespoons extra-virgin olive oil

3 tablespoons balsamic vinegar

1 tablespoon honey

Salt and freshly ground black pepper

2 large ripe yellow tomatoes,
    cut into $1/2$-inch slices

3 large ripe red tomatoes,
    cut into $1/2$-inch slices

2 large ripe orange tomatoes,
    cut into $1/2$-inch slices

3 medium-size zebra stripe or other heirloom
    tomatoes, cut into $1/2$-inch slices

$1/2$ pound assorted colored cherry
    tomatoes, halved

6 slices coarse-textured country-style
    bread, toasted

3 tablespoons finely snipped fresh chives,
    for garnish

Warm a skillet over medium-high heat. Add the pine nuts and cook, stirring constantly, until golden, 1 to 2 minutes. Remove from the pan and let cool. Place in a bowl with the butter and Gorgonzola and mash together with a fork. Reserve.

In a small bowl, whisk together the olive oil, vinegar, and honey to make a vinaigrette. Season to taste with salt and pepper. Reserve.

Ten minutes before serving, preheat the oven to 400°F. Alternate the slices of tomato on a serving plate. Sprinkle the cherry tomatoes over them. Season to taste with salt and pepper. Drizzle with the vinaigrette.

Spread the cheese mixture on the toasted bread. Place the bread on a baking sheet and bake on the top shelf of the oven until the bread is golden brown around the edges, 1 to 2 minutes. Cut the bread on the diagonal into 3-inch pieces. Place the Gorgonzola toasts around the edges of the serving plate. Sprinkle the salad and toasts with chives and serve immediately.

Serves 6

TO DRINK: Rosé

Firsts

feta and olive crostini

That leg of lamb you're grilling still has a little ways to go, but the natives are getting restless. Bring out this crostini with its zippy topping of olives, feta, roasted red peppers, garlic, and mint and you'll be amazed at how patient and content everyone will suddenly become. One little tip—mix the topping ingredients together gently just before serving. This will keep the colors and flavors vibrant and fresh.

24 baguette slices, cut diagonally
 $1/2$ inch thick

2 tablespoons extra-virgin olive oil

1 small red bell pepper, roasted and
 diced (page 6)

1 garlic clove, minced

2 teaspoons lemon juice

1 cup imported black olives (such as niçoise
 or kalamata), pitted and chopped

2 tablespoons chopped fresh flat-leaf parsley

$1^{1}/_{2}$ tablespoons chopped fresh mint

4 ounces feta cheese

Preheat the oven to 400°F.

Lightly brush both sides of the slices of bread with olive oil. Place the slices in a single layer on a baking sheet and bake, turning occasionally, until golden, 7 to 10 minutes.

In a bowl, mix together the red pepper, garlic, lemon juice, olives, parsley, and mint. Crumble the feta on top and mix gently just until combined.

Top each slice of bread with a tablespoon of the feta mixture and serve immediately.

Serves 8

TO DRINK: Prosecco

crostini with feta and hot red pepper

This is my very favorite kind of recipe, simple but absolutely full of pungent flavors—here feta, garlic, and cayenne pepper. I keep coming back to this recipe again and again because it takes all of five minutes to make, yet the results are astonishingly delicious. Rather than spreading it on a crostini as in the previous recipe, use it more like a dip. Note that the whole or skim yogurt must drain for four hours before using.

1 cup plain whole, skim, or
    Greek yogurt

$^1/_4$ teaspoon salt

10 ounces feta cheese

2 garlic cloves, minced

$^1/_2$ to $^3/_4$ teaspoon cayenne pepper

1 teaspoon sweet paprika

1 tablespoon plus 1 teaspoon
    extra-virgin olive oil

12 slices coarse-textured country-
    style bread

Imported black olives, for garnish

Drain the yogurt in a sieve lined with paper towels for 4 hours. (If you are using Greek yogurt, you don't have to drain it.) Place the drained yogurt, salt, and feta in a bowl and mash together with a fork to make a smooth paste. Add the garlic, cayenne, paprika, and 1 tablespoon of the olive oil and mix well. Alternately, this can be pureed in the food processor or blender.

Toast or grill the bread on both sides and cut into 2-inch pieces. Spread the puree on a serving plate. Drizzle with the remaining 1 teaspoon olive oil and garnish with the olives. Serve with the toasted bread.

Serves 6

TO DRINK: Grüner Veltliner, Pinot Grigio, Bianco di Custoza, or Soave

crostini with artichokes and olives

This may seem odd to you, adding grape leaves to a crostini. I first tasted it in Italy and loved the heady combination of artichokes, grape leaves, olives, garlic, and lemon. If you don't have access to fresh grape leaves, the jarred ones, available at supermarkets and specialty food stores, impart the same flavor. (Pictured opposite.)

6 whole artichokes in oil and brine,
    very coarsely chopped

4 grape leaves in brine, stems removed,
    rinsed, and very coarsely chopped

$1/2$ cup imported green olives
    (such as picholine), pitted

1 garlic clove, minced

$1/2$ teaspoon grated lemon zest

$1^1/2$ tablespoons extra-virgin olive oil

1 tablespoon lemon juice

Salt and freshly ground black pepper

16 baguette slices, cut diagonally
    $1/2$ inch thick

Lemon wedges, for garnish

In a bowl, combine the artichokes, grape leaves, olives, garlic, and lemon zest. Place on a cutting board and chop together until coarsely chopped. Return the mixture to the bowl and add the olive oil, lemon juice, and salt and pepper to taste. Toast or grill the bread on both sides.

To serve, spread the mixture onto the toasted bread and serve immediately, garnished with the lemon wedges.

Serves 8

TO DRINK: Champagne or sparkling wine

crostini with fennel sausage

This is the easiest recipe in the whole book, using the fewest ingredients. But don't let the simplicity of this dish fool you—the flavors are deep and satisfying. It's one of my favorites for entertaining. I always make more than I need so I can freeze the rest. Then, when friends drop by for a glass of wine all I have to do is defrost, spread, and bake.

$1/2$ pound hot Italian sausage,
    casings removed

5 ounces grated fontina or crumbled
    Robiola or Taleggio cheese

1 teaspoon fennel seed, coarsely ground

2 tablespoons chopped fresh
    flat-leaf parsley

Salt

12 slices rustic coarse-textured bread,
    cut into 2- to 3-inch serving pieces

Preheat the oven to 350°F.

Crumble the sausage into a bowl. Add the cheese, fennel seed, parsley, and salt to taste. Spread onto the bread, distributing evenly. Place in a single layer on a baking sheet. Bake in the oven until golden and crispy, 15 minutes.

Serves 6

TO DRINK: Sangiovese

wild mushroom and blue cheese crostini

You can find fresh wild mushrooms at the market during the fall and again after the spring rains. Combine their earthiness with blue-veined cheese and fontina to make a delicious crostini topping. At the last minute, slide them under the broiler until the cheese oozes and bubbles and the mushrooms are hot.

2 tablespoons extra-virgin olive oil

$^1/_2$ pound wild mushrooms, thinly sliced

$^1/_2$ pound cultivated mushrooms, thinly sliced

1 tablespoon chopped fresh flat-leaf parsley

1 teaspoon chopped fresh thyme

1 teaspoon chopped fresh mint

Salt and freshly ground black pepper

1 cup coarsely grated fontina cheese

$^1/_2$ cup crumbled Gorgonzola cheese

12 slices coarse-textured country-style bread

2 garlic cloves, peeled

2 tablespoons lemon juice, for drizzling

Whole leaves of fresh flat-leaf parsley,
    for garnish

In a large skillet over medium-high heat, heat the olive oil. Add the mushrooms and cook, stirring occasionally, until golden and the liquid has evaporated, 7 to 10 minutes. Add the parsley, thyme, and mint, and toss together. Season well with salt and pepper. Remove from the heat. Let cool and add both cheeses. Toss together.

Preheat the broiler.

Toast or grill the bread on both sides. Rub each side of the toast lightly with garlic. Distribute the mushroom-cheese mixture on top of the toasts. Place the toasts on a baking sheet in a single layer and broil until the cheese melts, about 1 minute. Transfer to a platter and drizzle with the lemon juice. Serve immediately, garnished with the parsley leaves.

Serves 6

TO DRINK: Nero d'Avola

crostini with beans and greens

Crostini is my standby when I am having company for dinner. It's substantial enough to stave off hunger and versatile enough that I can top it with just about anything. Besides, everybody likes good toasted bread with tasty things on top. Made with a mixture of mashed chickpeas, olive oil, and garlic topped with warm Swiss chard wilted in garlic-scented olive oil, these nibbles get a little spicy kick from the red pepper flakes. Note that the chickpeas must soak for at least four hours before using.

$3/4$ cup dried chickpeas

$1/4$ cup extra-virgin olive oil

1 garlic clove, minced, plus 3 cloves, crushed

Salt and freshly ground black pepper

1 large bunch Swiss chard, escarole, or beet or turnip greens,

2 garlic cloves, crushed

Large pinch of red pepper flakes

12 slices rustic country-style bread, cut into2- to 3-inch serving pieces

Pick over the chickpeas and discard any stones or damaged ones. Cover with cold water and soak for 4 hours or overnight.

Place the chickpeas in a saucepan with enough water to cover by 2 inches. Simmer, uncovered, over medium-low heat until the skins begin to crack and the peas are tender, 50 to 60 minutes. Drain, reserving $1/2$ cup of the cooking liquid. Cool the chickpeas in a bowl.

Puree the chickpeas in a blender or food processor with 2 tablespoons of the olive oil and as much of the reserved bean cooking liquid as needed to make a very thick paste. Add the minced garlic and season with salt and pepper. Reserve.

Remove the stems from the greens and cut the greens into 1-inch strips. Heat the remaining 2 tablespoons olive oil in a large skillet over low heat and cook the crushed garlic until golden. Remove and discard. Add the greens and cook, stirring occasionally, until the greens wilt, 3 to 4 minutes. Season with red pepper flakes, and salt and pepper.

Toast or grill the bread on both sides. Spread each slice with some of the chickpea puree and place a few leaves of the wilted greens on top of the beans. Serve immediately.

Serves 6

TO DRINK: Viognier or Sauvignon Blanc

anchovy and olive crusts

We all know people who would rather walk across hot coals than eat anything with anchovies. Convert them with this simple trick: soak the anchovies in cold water for ten minutes and pat them dry with paper towels. The anchovies will be rid of their strong, fishy flavor. Of course, anchovy lovers who try these will go crazy for this recipe.

8 anchovy fillets, boned

2 shallots, minced

$1/2$ cup imported black olives
    (such as niçoise or kalamata), pitted
    and chopped, plus some whole ones,
    for garnish

3 tablespoons extra-virgin olive oil

1 tablespoon red wine vinegar

4 garlic cloves, minced

$1/4$ cup chopped fresh flat-leaf parsley

Freshly ground black pepper

12 baguette slices, cut diagonally
    $1/4$ inch thick

Lemon wedges, for garnish

Whole baby radishes with their tops,
    for garnish

Place the anchovies in a bowl of cold water and let soak for 10 minutes. Drain and pat dry with paper towels. Chop the anchovies coarsely and place in a bowl. Add the shallots, chopped olives, and olive oil and stir together.

Place the mixture on a cutting board and chop until the anchovies, shallots, and olives are very finely chopped. Return the mixture to the bowl. Add the vinegar, garlic, and parsley. Season to taste with pepper.

Preheat the broiler.

Arrange the bread slices on a baking sheet and toast on both sides until golden. Spread the toasts with the anchovy mixture and broil just until warm, 30 to 60 seconds. Place the crusts on a platter and garnish with the lemon wedges, radishes, and whole olives. Serve immediately.

Serves 6

TO DRINK: Greco or Albarino

grilled bread with ripe tomatoes and olive oil

Picture this—thick slices of country-style bread toasted over a wood fire until lightly golden and smeared all over with a juicy, fleshy tomato. Drizzle with garlic-scented oil, sprinkle with coarse salt, and you have the best of summer, a favorite in Barcelona and at my house when I need a spur-of-the-moment taste sensation.

2 garlic cloves, peeled

Salt and freshly ground black pepper

1/4 cup extra-virgin olive oil

12 slices coarse-textured country-style
bread, sliced 3/4 inch thick

3 very ripe tomatoes

12 anchovy fillets, soaked in cold water
for 10 minutes and patted dry,
for garnish (optional)

6 paper-thin slices Serrano ham or
prosciutto, for topping (optional)

12 paper-thin slices Manchego cheese,
for topping (optional)

1/2 cup green or black imported olives,
for topping (optional)

Preheat a broiler or start a charcoal or wood fire.

Mince the garlic and then mash it with the side of a chef's knife or in a mortar and pestle with a large pinch of salt. Mix the garlic with the olive oil. Reserve for later.

Grill the bread until golden brown on both sides.

Cut the tomatoes in half and, cupping a tomato half in your palm with the cut side facing away from your palm, rub both sides of the toast with the tomato, squeezing slightly as you go along to leave pulp, seeds, and juice.

Drizzle the garlic olive oil on each side of the toast and sprinkle with salt and pepper. Place on a platter and garnish with anchovies, Serrano ham, and Manchego cheese, placing the anchovies, ham, and Manchego alternately on top of different pieces of bread. Scatter the olives between the pieces of bread and serve.

Serves 6

TO DRINK: Spanish Cava

charcoal-grilled oysters with sweet and hot red peppers

There's something ancient and deeply gratifying about watching oyster shells popping open over a fire. This is a simple dish to make, but the flavors are sweet, salt, sour, and smoky all in one bite. Serve these oysters on a bed of rock salt as a first course, with fresh rye bread slathered with sweet butter.

$1/2$ cup red wine, such as Cabernet Sauvignon, Merlot, or Zinfandel

3 tablespoons red wine vinegar

1 shallot, minced

$1/2$ red bell pepper, roasted and diced (page 6)

Pinch of red pepper flakes

Salt and freshly ground black pepper

Rock salt, for serving

2 dozen fresh oysters, in the shell

Buttered rye bread, for accompaniment

Heat a charcoal grill and adjust the rack so it is 1 inch above the coals.

In a small bowl, whisk together the red wine, red wine vinegar, shallot, red bell pepper, and red pepper flakes to make a sauce. Season to taste with salt and pepper.

In the meantime, spread 2 large ovenproof platters with about $1/2$ inch of rock salt. Place the oysters directly on the grill, curved side down. When the shells just open slightly and the oyster juices begin to bubble, 2 to 4 minutes, remove the oysters from the fire. Finish opening the oysters with an oyster knife and discard the top shell.

To serve, place the oysters on the rock salt in a single layer. Put a couple teaspoons of the sauce on each oyster and serve immediately with the buttered rye bread.

Serves 6

TO DRINK: Vouvray or white Rhône

warm grilled bread salad with fresh mozzarella

This is a cross between a salad and a crostini. It's colorful, bright, flavorful, and really healthy—everything a good dish should be all wrapped into one. Serve it in the fall as a first course for lamb chops or rib-eye steaks grilled over a charcoal fire.

2 Japanese eggplants, sliced diagonally
 1/4 inch thick

5 tablespoons extra-virgin olive oil

6 large slices coarse-textured
 country-style bread

2 garlic cloves, peeled

3 tablespoons lemon juice

4 anchovy fillets, boned, soaked in
 cold water for 10 minutes,
 patted dry, and mashed

1 shallot, minced

Salt and freshly ground black pepper

3/4 pound fresh cow's milk mozzarella
 cheese, thinly sliced

6 lemon wedges

12 baby radishes with fresh bright
 green leaves

24 imported black olives

1 recipe Artichokes Stewed with Olive Oil,
 Lemon, and Plenty of Garlic (page 176),
 for topping

1 red bell pepper, roasted and cut into
 1-inch strips (page 6), for topping

1 yellow bell pepper, roasted and cut into
 1-inch strips (page 6), for topping

Preheat the oven to 375°F.

Brush the eggplant slices with 1 tablespoon of the oil and place them in a single layer on a baking sheet. Bake on the top rack of the oven, turning occasionally, until golden, 15 to 18 minutes. Set aside to cool.

Cut each slice of bread into 2- to 2 1/2-inch wedges. Toast or grill the wedges until golden on both sides and rub each side with garlic.

In a small bowl, whisk together the lemon juice, anchovies, shallot, and remaining 4 tablespoons olive oil to make a dressing. Season with salt and pepper.

Place the toasted bread slices in a single layer on a baking sheet and top with the mozzarella, distributing the cheese evenly. Bake on the top rack of the oven until the mozzarella begins to melt, 1 to 2 minutes.

To serve, place 2 pieces of grilled bread on each plate. Drizzle a spoonful of the anchovy-lemon dressing on top. Garnish with the eggplant, lemon wedges, radishes, olives, artichokes, and roasted pepper strips, and serve immediately.

Serves 6

TO DRINK: Chianti

feta preserved in fruity virgin olive oil with summer herbs

You can make this pungent feta and store it in the refrigerator for up to three months. Just make sure the cheese is completely submerged in the olive oil. When you want a quick and easy appetizer, place the cheese on a pretty platter, and bring it to room temperature. Garnish the platter with kalamata olives, roasted red bell peppers, and caperberries. Don't forget a big basket of hot-from-the-oven pita bread.

3 sprigs of fresh oregano

1 sprig of fresh rosemary, plus 2 sprigs, for garnish

4 sprigs of fresh thyme

2 sprigs of fresh savory (optional)

1 cup extra-virgin olive oil, plus more for preserving

3/4 pound feta cheese

1 1/2 teaspoons chopped fresh oregano, for garnish

1/2 teaspoon chopped fresh thyme, for garnish

Pita bread, for accompaniment

With the spine of a chef's knife, tap the herb sprigs gently to bruise the stems slightly.

Warm 1 cup of the olive oil in a saucepan over medium heat. Add the oregano, rosemary, thyme, and savory sprigs and heat just until the herbs sizzle, 30 to 60 seconds. Remove from the heat and let cool.

Place half of the herbs and herb-scented oil in a 1-pint mason jar. Cut the feta to fit into the jar. Add the remaining herbs and oil to the jar. Add enough additional oil to cover the feta completely. Cover the jar and place in the refrigerator for a minimum of 2 weeks or up to 3 months.

To serve, bring the feta to room temperature, drain, and place on a platter. Discard the herb sprigs. Drizzle a few tablespoons of the oil over the cheese. Sprinkle with the chopped fresh oregano and thyme, garnish with the rosemary sprigs, and serve.

Serves 6

TO DRINK: Prosecco

soft mozzarella poached with tomatoes and basil

Imagine soft, creamy, melting buffalo mozzarella surrounded by a pool of sweet tomato and basil sauce. Buffalo mozzarella, or "mozzarella di bufala," is the most prized of fresh mozzarellas. Originally made in Southern Italy, today it is also made in the United States, often from a combination of water buffalo and cow's milk. If buffalo mozzarella is unavailable, try using cow's milk mozzarella, made and readily available in the United States. Serve it with bruschetta (toasted bread rubbed with a clove of garlic), drizzled with your best extra-virgin olive oil and sprinkled with fleur de sel. If the pieces of mozzarella you purchase are larger than 3 ounces each, cut them to size.

$^1/_4$ cup extra-virgin olive oil

4 garlic cloves, crushed

3 pounds tomatoes (fresh or canned), peeled, seeded, chopped, and drained (page 6)

Salt and freshly ground black pepper

6 small balls fresh buffalo mozzarella cheese (about 3 ounces each), drained, at room temperature

$^1/_2$ cup fresh basil leaves

Sprigs of basil, for garnish

Crusty bread, for accompaniment

Heat the oil in a large saucepan over medium heat. Add the garlic and cook, stirring, until the garlic is golden, about 2 minutes. Remove the garlic and discard. Decrease the heat to medium-low, add the tomatoes, and simmer until the tomatoes soften and begin to liquify. Season to taste with salt and pepper. Let cool for 10 minutes. Puree in a blender until smooth.

Twenty minutes before serving, bring the sauce to a simmer in a large saucepan over medium heat. Place the mozzarella in the sauce so that it is half submerged. Remove the pan from the heat and let sit for 6 to 8 minutes.

In the meantime, cut the basil leaves into thin strips.

To serve, place a piece of warm mozzarella on each plate. Stir the basil into the sauce. Spoon the sauce around the mozzarella. Garnish with the basil sprigs and serve immediately with the bread.

Serves 6

TO DRINK: Sangiovese

warm olives with fennel and orange

A glass of chilled Champagne or sparkling wine and a plate of warm olives studded with orange, fennel, and garlic is a perfect way to start any evening in the wine country. The briny, slightly salty flavor of the olives pairs well with a yeasty Champagne. Any leftovers? Place them in a mason jar and store in the refrigerator for up to a month. To serve, simply warm them gently on the stovetop.

2 oranges

1 medium-size fennel bulb, cut into eighths

$^3/_4$ cup extra-virgin olive oil

$^1/_2$ teaspoon fennel seed, coarsely cracked

4 garlic cloves, thinly sliced

$^1/_8$ teaspoon red pepper flakes

4 ounces niçoise olives

4 ounces green picholine olives

2 ounces oil-cured olives

2 ounces kalamata black olives

With a vegetable peeler, remove 8 strips of orange peel, each 2 inches long. Try not to remove any of the white pith. If there is white pith, scrape it off with a paring knife.

Bring a large pot of salted water to a boil over high heat. Add the fresh fennel and cook for 3 minutes. Remove from the heat and drain.

Warm the olive oil in a large saucepan over medium heat. Add the orange peel, fresh fennel, fennel seed, garlic, and red pepper flakes and cook until all begin to sizzle, about 1 minute. Add the olives and warm gently for 5 minutes. Remove from the heat and let sit for 6 hours. Discard the orange peel.

Ten minutes before serving, re-warm the olive mixture. To serve, place the olives and fennel on a small platter. Drizzle with a few tablespoons of the flavored oil and serve immediately.

Serves 6

TO DRINK: Champagne or sparkling wine

brown butter, walnut, and cheddar wafers

These homemade wafers are fun to serve with wine before a meal. The brown butter lends an extra-deep, nutty flavor. Make the cracker dough ahead of time and store it in the freezer. When you need crackers, slice and bake. Or bake them and store in an airtight container for up to a week.

6 tablespoons unsalted butter

1 cup grated extra-sharp cheddar cheese

1 tablespoon dry mustard

1/4 teaspoon cayenne pepper

1/2 teaspoon salt

1 cup all-purpose flour

1 teaspoon baking powder

1 large egg

1 teaspoon plus 2 tablespoons water

1/4 cup walnuts, toasted and
    finely ground (page 7)

Place the butter in a saucepan over medium-high heat. Cook until the butter melts and the tiny solids on the bottom turn brown and begin to smoke slightly, 2 to 3 minutes. Immediately remove from the heat.

Place the butter, cheese, mustard, cayenne, salt, flour, and baking powder in the bowl of a food processor. Process until well mixed and forms a dough, 1 to 2 minutes. Place the dough in a bowl, cover with plastic wrap, and chill in the refrigerator for 1 hour.

Divide the dough in half and form each piece into a 1-inch-diameter log. Wrap each log tightly in plastic wrap and roll to smooth the edges. Chill in the freezer for 20 minutes.

Preheat the oven to 350°F.

For the glaze, whisk the egg with the 1 teaspoon water.

Unwrap the dough and slice into 1/4-inch discs. Sprinkle a baking sheet with the 2 tablespoons water. Place the dough rounds on the baking sheet 1 inch apart. Brush with the glaze and sprinkle with the toasted walnuts. Bake until golden, about 15 minutes. Remove from the pan and let cool. Serve hot or at room temperature.

Makes 4 to 5 dozen crackers

TO DRINK: White Rioja

asparagus cheese puffs

These delightful little puffs are called gougères (rhymes with "blue hair") in France and are a favorite served with a glass of white wine before a meal. But the only way this recipe will appeal to everyone is if you use plenty of cheese, lots of fresh asparagus, a good dash of cayenne, and salt. Don't be shy with this one: serve them hot so they will melt in your mouth.

1/2 pound asparagus, ends trimmed

3/4 cup whole milk

5 tablespoons unsalted butter, cut into 10 pieces

1/2 teaspoon salt, plus more for the pot

3/4 cup all-purpose flour

1/4 teaspoon cayenne pepper

3 large eggs, at room temperature

1 cup coarsely grated dry sheep's milk cheese, such as pecorino or Manchego

1/2 cup finely grated Parmigiano-Reggiano cheese

Cut the asparagus into 1/4-inch lengths. Bring a medium saucepan of salted water to a boil over medium-high heat. Add the asparagus and simmer until just tender, about 1 minute. Drain immediately and reserve.

In a heavy saucepan, bring the milk and butter to a boil over medium-high heat. In the meantime, sift together the 1/2 teaspoon salt, flour, and cayenne. As soon as the milk comes to a boil and the butter has melted, remove the pan from the heat and add the flour mixture all at once. With a wooden spoon, beat the mixture until it thickens and pulls away from the sides of the pan, about 1 minute. Transfer the mixture to a bowl. Add the eggs, 1 at a time, beating well after each addition. Do not add another egg until the previous one has been thoroughly incorporated. Let cool for 10 minutes.

Preheat the oven to 400°F. Line 2 baking sheets with lightly buttered parchment paper.

Add the asparagus, sheep's milk cheese, and Parmigiano to the dough and mix together. Spoon rounded teaspoons of the dough 1 inch apart onto the baking sheets. Bake in the middle of the oven until golden brown, 20 to 25 minutes. Remove the puffs from the parchment and serve immediately.

Makes 36 puffs to serve 6

TO DRINK: Pouilly-Fumé

warm olive and caramelized onion tart

This free-form tart is a must when you have plenty of onions that you've pulled fresh from the vegetable garden or purchased from the farmer's market. The simple pastry, made in ten minutes from ice-cold butter and flour, is a variation on labor-intensive puff pastry. You cannot believe how simple this pastry is to make nor how wonderful the results are. After a 45-minute resting period, it's time to roll a perfect pastry for sweet caramelized onions, tomatoes, black olives, and anchovies.

1 cup all-purpose flour

$^1/_3$ cup cake flour

Salt and freshly ground black pepper

$^3/_4$ cup (1$^1/_2$ sticks) butter, cut into
$^1/_2$-inch cubes and frozen for 1 hour

$^1/_4$ cup ice water

3 tablespoons extra-virgin olive oil

5 medium-size yellow onions, thinly sliced

3 garlic cloves, chopped

1 teaspoon chopped fresh thyme

$^1/_2$ teaspoon chopped fresh rosemary

1 cup peeled, seeded, and chopped tomatoes
(fresh or canned) (page 6)

2 anchovy fillets, boned, soaked in cold water
for 10 minutes, patted dry, and mashed

$^1/_2$ cup imported black olives, pitted and
coarsely chopped

Combine the 2 flours in a bowl and freeze for 1 hour. On a cold work surface, mix the frozen flour with $^1/_2$ teaspoon salt. Add the frozen butter and cut into $^1/_4$-inch pieces with a metal pastry scraper. Add the ice water a little at a time until the mixture almost holds together.

On a lightly floured board, press the mixture together as best you can to form a rough rectangular shape. There will be large chunks of butter showing. Work quickly and do not knead. Roll out the dough into a $^1/_2$-inch-thick rectangle, about 5 by 7 inches. Fold the 2 narrow ends toward

the center to meet in the center. Fold in half again so that there are 4 layers. Turn the dough a quarter of a turn. This is your first turn. Roll again to form a $^1/_2$-inch-thick rectangle. Repeat the folding process. This is your second turn. Repeat the rolling and turning 1 more time. For the fourth turn, roll the dough and fold the dough into thirds as you would a business letter, wrap the dough in plastic wrap, and refrigerate for 45 to 60 minutes.

In the meantime, for the filling, warm the oil in a skillet over medium-low heat. Add the onions, garlic, thyme, and rosemary, and cook over low heat, stirring occasionally, until the onions are soft and golden, 50 to 60 minutes. Add the tomatoes and continue to cook until almost dry, 10 to 15 minutes. Stir in the anchovies and olives, season to taste with salt and pepper, and set aside to cool.

Preheat the oven to 400°F. On a floured surface, roll the dough $^1/_4$ inch thick to form a 13 by 9-inch rectangle. Crimp the edges. Place the dough on a baking sheet. Spread the onion mixture over the dough, leaving a $^1/_2$-inch border around the edge uncovered. Bake until the crust is golden and crisp, 30 to 40 minutes.

Serves 6

TO DRINK: Sparkling wine or a dry rosé

goat cheese and green onion galette

A galette is a fancy way of saying "a thin pie." This one has a crunchy dough, rich with butter, that is a perfect casing for creamy ricotta, crème fraîche, mozzarella, fresh green onions, and Parmigiano. You'll see why this has been one of my all-time favorites for years.

1 1/2 cups all-purpose flour

Salt and freshly ground black pepper

1/2 cup (1 stick) plus 1 tablespoon butter, cut into 1/2-inch pieces and chilled in the freezer for 1 hour

1/3 to 1/2 cup ice water

1 tablespoon extra-virgin olive oil

2 bunches green onions, white and green parts, thinly sliced

5 ounces goat cheese

4 ounces ricotta cheese

3/4 cup coarsely grated mozzarella cheese

1/4 cup crème fraîche

1/4 cup grated Parmigiano-Reggiano cheese

Put the flour in a bowl and chill in the freezer for 1 hour. Place the flour and 1/4 teaspoon salt on a cold work surface. With a pastry scraper, cut the frozen butter into the flour until half of the butter clumps are the size of peas and the rest are a little larger. Make a well in the center and add half of the ice water. Push together with your fingertips and set aside any dough that holds together. Add the rest of the water and repeat. Form the mixture into a rough ball.

Alternately, this can be made by judiciously pulsing the ingredients in a food processor, using the same technique, until half is the size of peas and the other half a little larger. Pour the mixture out onto your work surface and add the water as above. Do not add it into the food processor. Form the mixture into a rough ball. Or this can be made in an electric mixer using the same technique.

On a well-floured surface, roll out the dough into a 14-inch circle and trim the edges. Place on a large baking sheet and refrigerate.

Warm the olive oil in a large skillet over medium heat. Add the green onions and cook until soft, 4 to 5 minutes. Remove from the heat and let cool.

Mix together the green onions, goat cheese, ricotta, mozzarella, crème fraîche, and Parmigiano. Mix well and season with salt and pepper.

Preheat the oven to 375°F.

Remove the pastry from the refrigerator. Spread the cheese mixture over the pastry, leaving a 2 1/2-inch border around the edge uncovered. Fold the uncovered edge of the pastry over the cheese, pleating it to make it fit. The filling will be exposed in the center of the galette.

Bake the galette in the oven until golden brown, 35 to 40 minutes. Let cool for 5 minutes, then slide the galette off the pan and onto a serving plate. Serve hot, warm, or at room temperature.

Serves 6

TO DRINK: Sancerre, Rueda, or Grüner Veltliner

spicy corn soufflé

Summer is the time when you want to make this soufflé. Baked on a platter for only 15 to 20 minutes, this soufflé is packed with succulent sweet corn, spicy hot jalapeño, and melted fontina cheese. It can be served as a first course or a light main course, but this golden beauty does need to be gobbled up as soon as it's pulled from the oven.

10 ears fresh corn, shucked

3 cups half-and-half

$^1/_4$ cup ($^1/_2$ stick) unsalted butter,
    plus more for coating

5 tablespoons all-purpose flour

6 large eggs, separated

1 red pepper, roasted and diced (page 6)

1 small jalapeño pepper, seeded and diced

$^1/_2$ teaspoon sweet paprika

Pinch of cayenne pepper

1 cup grated fontina cheese

Salt and freshly ground black pepper

Slice the kernels of corn off the cob and reserve. Cut each corncob into a few pieces and place in a saucepan with the half-and-half and half of the reserved corn kernels. Bring to a simmer over low heat and simmer for 2 minutes. Remove from the heat. Remove the corncobs from the pan and scrape the cobs with the blunt side of a knife to remove all of the half-and-half and corn juices from the cobs. Add these scrapings to the half-and-half and corn. Discard the cobs. Puree this mixture in a blender and strain through a medium-mesh strainer.

Melt the 4 tablespoons butter in a saucepan over medium heat. Add the flour and stir con-stantly for 2 minutes. Add the scalded pureed corn mixture and stir until it thickens, 3 to 4 minutes. Transfer to a large bowl.

Preheat the oven to 450°F and set the top oven rack at the top third of the oven. Generously butter the bottom and low sides of a 15-inch square ovenproof platter (or two 12-inch ovals).

Add the egg yolks to the pureed cream mix-ture, 1 at a time, stirring well after each addition. Fold in the reserved corn, roasted red pepper, jala-peño, paprika, and cayenne. Fold in the cheese. Season with salt and pepper.

Place the egg whites in a clean bowl and beat until stiff peaks form. Fold one-quarter of the whites into the egg-yolk mixture with as few strokes as possible. Then fold in the remaining whites. Pour the mixture into the prepared plat-ter. Bake on the top rack of the oven until puffed and golden brown, 15 to 20 minutes.

Serve absolutely immediately!

Serves 6

TO DRINK: Albarino or dry Riesling

rice "olives"

I bet you can't eat just one. I got this recipe from the Feron family, who grow rice in the Veneto region of northern Italy. Gabrielle Feron likes to serve these bite-size antipasti—crisp on the outside and creamy inside—with a glass of wine before dinner. Olive paste can be purchased from any well-stocked market or you can make it yourself: place pitted kalamata or niçoise olives in a food processor and pulse until you have a coarse paste. As an alternative to olive paste, try using an equal amount of sun-dried tomato paste. Arborio, a short-grain Italian rice, is traditionally used for making risotto.

2 tablespoons extra-virgin olive oil

$^1/_2$ small yellow onion, minced

1 cup Arborio rice

$1^1/_4$ cups chicken stock

$1^1/_4$ cups whole milk

$^2/_3$ cup black olive paste

Salt and freshly ground black pepper

$^1/_4$ cup finely grated Parmigiano-
    Reggiano cheese

1 cup all-purpose flour

4 large eggs

$^1/_2$ cup water

4 cups toasted fresh bread crumbs,
    finely ground

Mixture of vegetable and olive oils, for frying

Heat the 2 tablespoons olive oil in a skillet over medium heat. Add the onion and sauté until soft, about 7 minutes. Add the rice and continue to cook, stirring constantly, for 2 minutes.

Place the chicken stock and milk in a saucepan and heat just to a simmer over low heat. Immediately add to the rice mixture along with $^1/_3$ cup of the olive paste and salt and pepper. Bring to a simmer, decrease the heat to low, cover, and cook slowly until the rice is cooked, about 20 minutes. Add the remaining $^1/_3$ cup olive paste and the Parmigiano. Let cool completely.

Form the mixture into small olive-size balls using less than 1 tablespoon of mixture for each. Place the flour in a bowl. Whisk together the eggs and the water in another bowl. Place the bread crumbs in a third bowl. Roll the rice "olives" in the flour, then the egg, then the bread crumbs. Place on a baking sheet until you are ready to cook them.

Heat 1 inch of oil in a deep pan to 375°F. Fry the rice "olives" until golden on all sides, 60 to 90 seconds. Remove and serve immediately.

Makes 60 balls, approximately 1 inch in diameter, to serve 12

TO DRINK: Prosecco

artichoke fritters with lemon mayonnaise

Use Meyer lemons, which are sweeter and less acidic than regular lemons, to make a particularly mellow mayonnaise that should be used the day it is made. It'll disappear quickly with crispy golden artichoke fritters!

LEMON MAYONNAISE

1 large egg yolk

1 teaspoon Dijon mustard

1/2 cup extra-virgin olive oil

1/2 cup peanut, vegetable, corn, or safflower oil

2 garlic cloves, minced or mashed

Juice of 1 Meyer lemon

Salt and freshly ground black pepper

2 to 3 tablespoons warm water

FRITTERS

1 cup plus 2 tablespoons all-purpose flour

Salt and freshly ground black pepper

2 teaspoons grated lemon zest

2 large eggs, separated, yolks beaten

3 tablespoons extra-virgin olive oil

Juice of 1 lemon

3/4 cup warm beer

6 large artichokes

1/2 cup water

Corn or peanut oil, for deep-frying

Whole leaves of fresh flat-leaf parsley,
     for garnish

To make the mayonnaise, in a small bowl, whisk together the egg yolk, mustard, and 1 tablespoon of the olive oil to form an emulsion. Combine the remaining olive oil and the peanut oil. Drop by drop, add the oil, whisking constantly. Do not add the oil too quickly and make sure that the emulsion is homogeneous before adding more oil. Season with garlic, lemon juice, and salt and pepper. Thin the mayonnaise the water.

To make the fritters, sift the flour and 1/2 teaspoon salt together in a bowl. Stir in the zest.

Make a well in the center and add the beaten egg yolks, 1 tablespoon of the olive oil, 1 tablespoon of the lemon juice, and the beer. Mix well with a whisk and let rest for 1 hour at room temperature.

Meanwhile, have ready a large bowl of water to which you have added the remaining lemon juice. Cut off the top half of the artichokes, including all of the prickly leaf points. Remove the tough outer leaves of the artichoke until you get to the very light green leaves. Pare the stem to reveal the light green center. Halve each artichoke lengthwise, then scoop out the prickly chokes and discard. Cut the artichokes into thin wedges lengthwise, placing each wedge into the bowl with lemon water.

Warm the remaining 2 tablespoons olive oil in a skillet over medium heat. Drain the artichokes and add to the pan with the water and a large pinch of salt and pepper. Cover and cook until the liquid evaporates, about 15 minutes. Let cool.

In a deep saucepan, add corn oil to a depth of 2 inches. Heat to 375°F when tested with a thermometer or until a drop of the batter sizzles on contact. Meanwhile, in a bowl, beat the egg whites until stiff. Gently fold the egg whites and artichokes into the batter.

Drop the mixture by heaping tablespoons into the hot oil; do not overcrowd the pan. Fry, turning often, until golden brown, about 2 minutes. Using a slotted spoon, transfer to paper towels to drain.

To serve, arrange the hot fritters on a platter. Garnish with the mayonnaise and parsley.

Serves 6 (makes 1 cup mayonnaise)

TO DRINK: Sauvignon Blanc or Grüner Veltliner

crispy polenta cakes with wild mushroom ragout

In the fall, after the grapes are harvested and there's a chill in the air, all kinds of wild mushrooms are available at the farmer's market. Buy dry, unblemished mushrooms to use in this rustic, earthy dish of crispy polenta cakes topped with mixed wild mushrooms.

$^1/_4$ cup ($^1/_2$ stick) unsalted butter, plus more for coating the pan, at room temperature

6 cups water

Salt and freshly ground black pepper

1 cup coarse polenta

$^1/_2$ cup grated Parmigiano-Reggiano cheese

2 tablespoons chopped fresh flat-leaf parsley

2 garlic cloves, minced

2 teaspoons extra-virgin olive oil

1 pound button or mixed fresh wild mushrooms, trimmed and sliced

3 cups chicken stock

$^1/_2$ cup heavy cream

2 cups all-purpose flour, for dusting

Olive or canola oil, for frying

Butter a 9 by 9-inch baking pan.

Bring the water and 1 teaspoon salt to a boil in a pot over medium-high heat. Decrease the heat to medium and slowly add the polenta in a shower, whisking constantly until the mixture thickens, 3 to 5 minutes. Change to a wooden spoon and continue to simmer, stirring occasionally, until the spoon stands in the polenta, 15 to 25 minutes. Add the Parmigiano and 2 tablespoons of the butter and mix well. Season with salt and pepper.

Immediately spread the polenta in the prepared pan. Smooth the top with a rubber spatula and refrigerate. The polenta can stay refrigerated for several hours or overnight. Combine the pars-ley and garlic and chop together until very fine. Reserve.

For the ragout, in a large skillet, melt the remaining 2 tablespoons butter with the extra-virgin olive oil over high heat. Add the mushrooms and cook, stirring occasionally, until golden and the mushroom liquid has evaporated, 7 to 10 minutes. Remove the mushrooms and set aside. Add the chicken stock, cream, and garlic-parsley mixture to the pan and simmer over medium-low heat until reduced by half, 6 to 8 minutes. Season with salt and pepper.

Score the polenta into six 3 by $4^1/_2$-inch squares. Halve each square diagonally to make 2 triangles. Remove the polenta triangles from the pan and toss them carefully in flour to dust them lightly.

Heat $^1/_2$ inch of olive or canola oil in a large, deep skillet until the oil sizzles and a tiny piece of polenta turns golden on contact, 375°F. Add the polenta triangles in batches—a few at a time—and cook, turning occasionally, until golden on both sides. Drain on paper towels.

To serve, place 2 hot polenta triangles on each plate. Warm the mushroom ragout and spoon over the polenta. Serve immediately.

Serves 6

TO DRINK: Rioja, red Burgundy, or Chianti

Pizza and Flatbread

parmigiano and black peppercorn breadsticks

Most Americans think of breadsticks as tasteless, pencil-thin sticks of toast wrapped in waxy envelopes, used mostly for decoration at Italian restaurants. But when homemade breadsticks are flavored with Parmigiano, a good dose of coarsely cracked black peppercorns, and cayenne, and served hot from the oven, trust me—it's a whole different experience. Serve them with cocktails or as an accompaniment to soups, salads, and, of course, a selection of your favorite antipasti.

2 teaspoons active dry yeast

$3^1/2$ cups unbleached bread flour

$1^1/2$ cups warm (110°F) water

2 teaspoons salt

$2^1/2$ tablespoons coarsely ground black pepper

$^1/4$ teaspoon cayenne pepper

2 tablespoons extra-virgin olive oil,
    plus more for brushing

1 cup finely grated Parmigiano-Reggiano cheese

$^1/2$ cup semolina flour

In a bowl, stir together the yeast, $^1/2$ cup of the flour, and $^1/2$ cup of the warm water. Let stand until the mixture bubbles and rises slightly, 30 minutes. Add the remaining 3 cups flour, the remaining 1 cup warm water, salt, black pepper, cayenne, and the 2 tablespoons olive oil, and stir together to form a ball. Knead on a lightly floured surface, kneading in the Parmigiano gradually, until smooth and elastic, 7 to 10 minutes. Alternately, this can be made in an electric mixer on slow speed using the dough hook, kneading for 5 minutes.

Using your hands, shape the dough into a 15 by 5-inch rectangle. Brush with olive oil, cover loosely with plastic wrap, and let rise in a warm place (about 75°F), until doubled in volume, 1 to $1^1/4$ hours.

Place a pizza stone on the bottom rack of the oven and preheat to 450°F.

Punch down the dough and sprinkle both sides of the dough with the semolina. On a floured surface, cut the dough into 5 equal 1-inch strips lengthwise. Cut the dough crosswise into 5 sections. This will make 25 pieces. Pick up each piece of dough and roll and stretch to fit the width of a baking sheet, about 8 to 10 inches long. Place in a single layer, 1 inch apart, on an oiled baking sheet. Bake on the middle rack of the oven until light golden, 10 to 12 minutes. Remove the breadsticks from the baking sheet and place directly onto the baking stone and bake until golden and crisp, 3 to 5 minutes. Remove from the oven and cool on a cooling rack.

Makes 25 breadsticks

TO DRINK: Barbera or Grüner Veltliner

focaccia with creamy taleggio

This is an Italian version of a grilled cheese sandwich. Creamy Taleggio cheese is sandwiched between two slices of focaccia dough, and baked to golden perfection on a pizza stone. When you cut the focaccia into wedges, the creamy cow's milk cheese oozes out of the center. Serve it hot from the oven.

2 teaspoons active dry yeast
$1^1/4$ cups warm (110°F) water
3 tablespoons extra-virgin olive oil
3 cups unbleached bread flour
Salt
12 ounces Taleggio cheese, coarsely grated
$1/3$ cup finely grated aged pecorino cheese

In a bowl, whisk together the yeast and $1/4$ cup of the water and let sit until creamy, about 20 minutes. Add the remaining 1 cup water, the olive oil, flour, and $1/2$ teaspoon salt. Knead on a lightly floured surface until smooth and soft, 7 to 8 minutes. Place in a well-oiled bowl and turn the dough over to coat the dough. Cover with plastic wrap and let the dough rise in a warm place (about 75°F) until it doubles in volume, about $1^1/2$ hours.

Place a pizza stone or tiles on the bottom rack of the oven. Heat the oven to 500°F for at least 30 minutes.

Punch down the dough, divide it into 4 pieces, and form each piece into a round ball. On a well-floured surface, roll 1 piece of dough into a 9-inch circle, $1/8$ inch thick. Transfer to a well-floured pizza peel. In a bowl, mix together the Taleggio and pecorino. Spread half of the cheese mixture on the dough, leaving a 1-inch border. Brush the edges of the dough lightly with water. Roll another ball to the same size and place on top. Crimp the edges to seal well. Pinch a hole in the center of the top piece of dough.

Transfer the focaccia to the hot pizza stone and bake until light golden and crisp, 7 to 10 minutes. Repeat with the remaining dough and cheese filling, making 1 more focaccia. Cut into wedges and serve immediately.

Serves 10

TO DRINK: Barbaresco

flatbread with roasted shallots and garlic

Caramelizing shallots and garlic with a little sugar really brings out their sweetness. Simmering them in wine adds a nice acidic counter note. Top the dough with this delicious mixture and you have a flatbread that your friends and family will really love, served alongside soups, stews, or solo, for munching. Forget the jasmine-scented candles: bake some of this delicious bread and your home will smell heavenly for hours.

DOUGH

2 1/2 teaspoons active dry yeast

2 1/2 cups unbleached bread flour

1 cup warm (110°F) water

1/4 cup extra-virgin olive oil

1 teaspoon chopped fresh rosemary

1 teaspoon salt

TOPPING

2 tablespoons extra-virgin olive oil

25 small shallots

20 garlic cloves

2 tablespoons sugar

3 cups dry red wine, such as Dolcetto or Barbera

Coarse salt and freshly ground black pepper

To make the dough, in a large bowl, mix together the yeast, 1/2 cup of the flour, and 1/2 cup of the warm water. Let stand until the mixture bubbles up, about 30 minutes. Add the remaining 2 cups flour, the remaining 1/2 cup water, olive oil, rosemary, and salt. Mix the dough thoroughly and knead on a floured board until soft, yet still moist, 7 to 8 minutes. Place the dough in an oiled bowl, turning once. Cover the bowl with plastic wrap and set aside in a warm place (about 75°F) until doubled in volume, 1 to 1 1/2 hours.

For the topping, heat the olive oil in a large skillet over medium-high heat. Add the shallots and garlic and cook, uncovered, stirring occasionally, until the shallots are golden brown, about 10 minutes. Add the sugar, stir well, and cook until the sugar caramelizes, about 4 minutes. Add 2 cups of the wine, cover, and simmer over low heat until the onions are soft, 20 to 25 minutes. Remove the cover, add the remaining 1 cup wine, and continue to simmer until the wine has evaporated, 10 to 15 minutes. Season with salt and pepper. Let the mixture cool.

Thirty minutes before baking, place a pizza stone on the bottom rack of the oven and preheat to 500°F.

Punch down the dough. On a floured surface, form the dough into a ball. Let rest for 5 minutes. Roll the dough into a 9 by 12-inch oval, 1/2 inch thick. Transfer to a well-floured pizza peel. Distribute the shallots and garlic on top of the flatbread and press them into the dough slightly. Sprinkle with coarse salt. Slide the flatbread onto the pizza stone and bake until golden brown and crisp, 12 to 15 minutes.

Serves 6

TO DRINK: Dolcetto or Barbera

crispy cracker bread

I am a sucker for good bread, so when I heard about the paper-thin, unleavened, crisp bread that Sardinia is famous for, in the name of research I just had to investigate. One bite, and I knew I had to learn to make it. I love this bread hot from the oven, drizzled with extra-virgin olive oil and scattered with aromatic rosemary needles.

3 cups unbleached bread flour

1^1/$_2$ cups fine semolina flour

1^1/$_2$ teaspoons salt

1^1/$_2$ to 1^3/$_4$ cups warm (110°F) water

2 teaspoons fresh rosemary needles (optional)

Coarse salt (optional)

In a bowl, mix together the flour, semolina, and salt. Add the water slowly to form a ball, making sure that the dough isn't too sticky or elastic. If the dough is sticky, dust it with flour. Divide the dough into 15 equal pieces. Form them into small balls without working them too much and place on a floured baking sheet. Cover with plastic wrap and set aside in a warm place (about 75°F) for 30 minutes.

Preheat the oven to 400°F. Place a pizza stone on the bottom rack of the oven and heat for at least 30 minutes.

Place 1 piece of dough on a floured surface. Flatten with the palm of your hand. Dust the top with flour. Roll the dough into a very thin circle, 8 to 10 inches in diameter and less than ^{1}/$_{16}$ inch thick. Place 1 at a time on a well-floured pizza peel and transfer to the pizza stone. Bake until it begins to blister, 2 to 3 minutes. Turn the bread over and continue to bake until it is golden and crisp, about 2 minutes. Watch the bread closely, because it burns quickly. Cool on a rack and continue to bake the remaining breads. Sprinkle with rosemary and coarse salt.

Serve warm in a large basket.

Serves 8

TO DRINK: Sparkling wine

wine country flatbread with grapes and toasted walnuts

If it's a good year for grape growing, that usually means a surplus. What do you do with all of those extra grapes? Make this flatbread topped with grapes of all different kinds—Chardonnay, Pinot Noir, and tiny green Champagne grapes. If these aren't available, simply substitute whatever green or red grapes you can find. If they are too large, cut them in half. The top of the flatbread is drizzled with fruity extra-virgin olive oil and coarse salt. It's sweet, it's hot from the oven, and it's everything a great flatbread should be.

3 sprigs of fresh rosemary

1/4 cup extra-virgin olive oil

1 tablespoon active dry yeast

2 cups unbleached bread flour

3/4 cup warm (110°F) water

1 tablespoon anise seed, coarsely ground

1/2 teaspoon salt

2 tablespoons sugar

1/2 cup walnuts, toasted and very
    coarsely chopped (page 7)

1 1/2 cups grapes (any variety)

1 teaspoon coarse salt, for sprinking

With the spine of a chef's knife, tap the rosemary sprigs gently to bruise the stems slightly. Heat the olive oil and rosemary in a skillet over medium heat until the rosemary sizzles, about 2 minutes. Remove from the heat and let cool. Remove the rosemary sprigs.

In a small bowl, stir together the yeast, 1/4 cup of the flour, and 1/4 cup of the water. Let stand until the mixture bubbles, 30 minutes. Add the anise seed, salt, sugar, remaining 1 3/4 cups flour, remaining 1/2 cup water, walnuts, and rosemary oil. Mix the ingredients together thoroughly with a wooden spoon. Turn the mixture out onto a floured board and knead until the dough is smooth and elastic, 7 to 8 minutes. Place the dough in a well-oiled bowl and turn it over to oil the top. Cover with plastic wrap and let rise in a warm place (about 75°F) until doubled in volume, 1 to 1 1/2 hours.

Thirty minutes before baking, preheat the oven to 450°F. Place a pizza stone on the bottom rack of the oven and heat for at least 30 minutes.

After the dough has doubled in volume, punch it down to deflate the bubbles. On a heavily floured surface, roll the dough to an 8 by 10-inch oval, 1/2 inch thick. Transfer to a well-floured pizza peel. With your fingertips, make slight dimples in the dough. Press the grapes into the top and sprinkle with the coarse salt. Slide the flatbread onto the pizza stone and bake until golden and crisp, 12 to 15 minutes.

Serve hot, warm, or at room temperature.

Serves 6

TO DRINK: Gewürztraminer

pizza dough

If you're already investing the extra effort to make your own dough from scratch, use Guisto's pizza flour or Caputo's "Tipo 00" flour, both available online. The flavor and perfectly chewy texture it produces will make you swear you're in Naples, except you'll only have to travel as far as your kitchen.

2 teaspoons active dry yeast

$^3/_4$ cup plus 2 tablespoons warm
    (110°F) water

2 cups unbleached bread flour

1 tablespoon extra-virgin olive oil

$^1/_2$ teaspoon salt

In a bowl, combine the yeast, $^1/_4$ cup of the warm water, and $^1/_4$ cup of the flour. Let stand for 30 minutes. Add the remaining $1^3/_4$ cups flour, the remaining $^1/_2$ cup plus 2 tablespoons warm water,
olive oil, and salt. Mix the dough thoroughly and turn out onto a floured surface. Knead until smooth, elastic, and a bit tacky to the touch, 7 to 8 minutes. Place in an oiled bowl and turn to coat. Cover with plastic wrap and let rise in a warm place (about 75°F) until doubled in volume, 1 to $1^1/_2$ hours. Or let the dough rise in the refrigerator overnight. The next day, let it come to room temperature and proceed with the recipe.

Makes two 10- to 11-inch pizzas

calzone dough

Calzones look difficult and complicated, but they are actually easy to make. Once you get the hang of pizza making, calzones are a snap. It's pretty much the same dough, but instead of baking the dough flat, you fill it with your favorite filling, fold it in half, seal it, and bake it.

2 teaspoons active dry yeast

1 cup warm (110°F) water

3 cups unbleached bread flour

$^3/_4$ teaspoon salt

2 tablespoons extra-virgin olive oil

Combine the yeast, $^1/_2$ cup of the water, and $^1/_2$ cup of the flour in a large bowl. Let it sit until it bubbles up, about 30 minutes. Add the remaining $2^1/_2$ cups flour, salt, olive oil, and the remaining $^1/_2$ cup water. Mix the dough thoroughly. Turn
out onto a floured surface and knead until smooth, elastic, and a bit tacky to the touch, 7 to 8 minutes. Place in an oiled bowl and turn to coat. Cover with plastic wrap and let rise in a warm place (about 75°F) until doubled in volume, 1 to $1^1/_2$ hours. Or you can let this dough rise in the refrigerator overnight. The next day, bring the dough to room temperature and proceed with the recipe.

Makes 2 large or 4 individual-size calzones

pizza margherita

This classic pizza is absolutely the best way to find out whether the *pizzaiolo* (pizza maker, in Italian) knows what he's doing. It's a basic pizza, but it showcases the quality and flavors of the crust, the cheese, and the rich tomato sauce. If you can find San Marzano canned tomatoes from Italy, by all means get them. They have the perfect combination of sweetness and acidity. Don't forget a few pieces of freshly torn basil leaves on top to incorporate more flavor and the three colors of the Italian flag—red, green, and white. *Mangia!*

1 recipe Pizza Dough (opposite page)
1 cup canned crushed tomatoes
    (preferably San Marzano)
Large pinch of dried oregano
Salt and freshly ground black pepper
16 fresh basil leaves
5 ounces buffalo mozzarella, thinly sliced
2 tablespoons extra-virgin olive oil

Make the pizza dough and let rise.

Thirty minutes before baking, preheat the oven to 500°F. Place a pizza stone on the bottom rack of the oven and heat for at least 30 minutes.

In a bowl, stir together the tomatoes and oregano. Season with salt and pepper.

Punch down the dough. On a floured surface, divide the dough into 2 pieces and form into balls. Do not work the dough too much. Roll 1 piece of dough into a 10- to 11-inch circle, $^3/_8$ inch thick. Transfer to a heavily floured pizza peel. Spread half of the tomato sauce on top of the dough, leaving a $^1/_2$-inch border around the edge. Tear 4 of the basil leaves into small pieces and sprinkle onto the tomato sauce, distributing evenly. Place half of the mozzarella on top of the basil, distributing evenly. Transfer the unbaked pizza directly onto the hot pizza stone and bake until golden and crisp, about 10 minutes.

Remove the pizza from the oven, drizzle with half of the olive oil, and top with 4 whole leaves of basil. Serve immediately. Repeat with the remaining ingredients to make a second pizza.

Makes two 10- to 11-inch pizzas, to serve 6 as an appetizer or 2 as a main course

TO DRINK: Prosecco, Champagne, sparkling wine, or Pinot Grigio

pizza with shrimp and spicy hot garlic mayonnaise

One great thing about pizzas is their versatility. You can top them with just about any flavor combination. I bake this pizza with fontina and mozzarella cheeses, and halfway through the cooking I add the shrimp. When the pizza is done, I drizzle the surface with garlic mayonnaise and watch it melt onto the toppings. I have also made this pizza with rings of fresh calamari with equally delicious results.

1 recipe Pizza Dough (page 100)

2 tablespoons extra-virgin olive oil

$^{1}/_{4}$ teaspoon red pepper flakes

2 garlic cloves, minced

$^{3}/_{4}$ cup coarsely grated fontina cheese

$^{3}/_{4}$ cup coarsely grated mozzarella cheese

$^{1}/_{3}$ cup prepared or homemade mayonnaise (page 87, substituting Eureka or Lisbon lemons for the Meyer lemons)

$^{1}/_{4}$ cup lemon juice

Salt and freshly ground black pepper

1 to 2 tablespoons water

$^{1}/_{2}$ small red onion, very thinly sliced

5 ounces peeled medium-size shrimp, cut in half lengthwise

1 tablespoon minced fresh green onions or chives, for garnish

Make the pizza dough and let rise.

Thirty minutes before baking, preheat the oven to 500°F. Place a pizza stone on the bottom rack of the oven and heat for at least 30 minutes.

In a bowl, combine the olive oil, red pepper flakes, and half of the garlic. Let stand for 30 minutes. In another bowl, combine the fontina and mozzarella and set aside.

Whisk the mayonnaise with the remaining garlic and the lemon juice. Season to taste with salt and pepper. Whisk in the water to make the mayonnaise a pourable consistency. Reserve the mayonnaise in the refrigerator.

Punch down the dough. On a floured surface, divide the dough into 2 pieces and form into balls. Roll 1 piece into a 9-inch circle, $^{1}/_{4}$ inch thick. Transfer to a well-floured pizza peel. Brush the dough to within $^{1}/_{2}$ inch of the edge with the garlic-infused oil. Sprinkle half of the cheese mixture over the dough. Top with half of the onions, distributing evenly. Slide the pizza onto the pizza stone and bake until the edges just start to turn golden, 3 to 4 minutes. Remove the pizza from the oven, top with half of the shrimp, distributing evenly in a single layer, and continue to bake until the pizza is golden and crisp and the shrimp have curled, 5 to 8 minutes. Drizzle with half of the mayonnaise, garnish with half of the green onions, and serve immediately.

Make a second pizza with the remaining ingredients.

Makes two 10- to 11-inch pizzas, to serve 6 as an appetizer or 2 as a main course

TO DRINK: Pinot Blanc or Chardonnay

pizza with asparagus, prosciutto, and truffle oil

Asparagus, truffles, and prosciutto—the combination is refined and delicious. If price is no object and truffles are in season, try shaving a few paper-thin slices of truffle—black or white—onto the top of the pizza in place of the truffle oil just before serving. The truffles will add an indescribably delicious blast of flavor.

1 recipe Pizza Dough (page 100)

1 garlic clove, minced

2 tablespoons extra-virgin olive oil

$^3/_4$ cup coarsely grated mozzarella cheese

$^3/_4$ cup coarsely grated fontina cheese

8 to 10 asparagus spears (about 6 ounces), ends trimmed and cut diagonally into $^1/_2$-inch pieces

Salt

6 paper-thin slices prosciutto, cut into 1-inch strips

2 tablespoons truffle oil

Make the pizza dough and let rise.

Thirty minutes before baking, preheat the oven to 500°F. Place a pizza stone on the bottom rack of the oven and heat for at least 30 minutes.

In a bowl, combine the garlic and olive oil and let stand for 30 minutes. In another bowl, combine the mozzarella and fontina and set aside.

Bring a saucepan of salted water to a boil over medium-high heat. Add the asparagus and cook until just tender, 3 to 4 minutes. Drain and cool.

Punch down the dough. On a floured surface, divide the dough into 2 pieces and form into balls. Roll 1 piece into a 9-inch circle, $^1/_4$ inch thick. Transfer to a well-floured pizza peel. Brush the dough to within $^1/_2$ inch of the edge with the garlic-infused oil. Sprinkle half of the cheese mixture over the dough. Top with half of the asparagus, distributing evenly. Sprinkle with salt. Slide the pizza onto the pizza stone and bake until golden and crisp, 8 to 12 minutes. Top with half of the prosciutto, distributing evenly. Drizzle with half of the truffle oil and serve immediately.

Make a second pizza with the remaining ingredients.

Makes two 10- to 11-inch pizzas, to serve 6 as an appetizer or 2 as a main course

TO DRINK: Greco di Tufo

pizza with wilted escarole, toasted pine nuts, and niçoise olives

Not all pizzas are topped with tomatoes. This one is covered with wilted escarole or other hearty greens flavored with red pepper flakes and a splash of balsamic vinegar, toasted pine nuts, and niçoise olives. It's salty, sweet, bitter, and sour, all in one bite. Swiss chard can stand in nicely for the escarole, if you prefer.

1 recipe Pizza Dough (page 100)
2 garlic cloves, minced
1/4 cup extra-virgin olive oil
3 ounces mozzarella cheese, grated
3 ounces fontina cheese, grated
1/4 cup pine nuts
1 head escarole, cut into 1-inch strips
1 tablespoon balsamic vinegar
Pinch of red pepper flakes
Salt and freshly ground pepper
1/2 cup pitted niçoise olives, coarsely chopped

Make the pizza dough and let rise.

Thirty minutes before baking, preheat the oven to 500°F. Place a pizza stone on the bottom rack of the oven and heat for at least 30 minutes.

In a bowl, combine the garlic and 2 tablespoons of the olive oil and let stand for 30 minutes. In another bowl, combine the mozzarella and fontina and set aside.

Warm a large skillet over medium-high heat. Add the pine nuts and cook, stirring occasionally, until golden, 1 to 2 minutes. Remove from the pan and reserve. Heat the remaining 2 tablespoons olive oil in the skillet over medium heat. Add the escarole and cook, stirring occasionally, until it wilts, 1 to 2 minutes. Add the balsamic vinegar and red pepper flakes. Season with salt and pepper.

Punch down the dough. On a floured surface, divide the dough into 2 pieces and form into balls. Do not work the dough too much. Roll 1 piece of dough into a 10- to 11-inch circle, 3/8 inch thick. Transfer to a heavily floured pizza peel and brush the dough to within 1/2 inch of edge with the garlic-infused oil. Sprinkle half the cheese mixture over the dough. Top with half each of the escarole, pine nuts, and olives, distributing evenly. Slide the unbaked pizza directly onto the pizza stone and bake until golden and crisp, 10 to 12 minutes.

Repeat with the remaining ingredients to make a second pizza.

Makes two 10- to 11-inch pizzas, to serve 6 as an appetizer or 2 as a main course

TO DRINK: Falanghina or Greco di Tufo

pizza with smoked trout and caviar

I call this one my "celebration pizza" because I always serve this one with Champagne for a special occasion. In place of smoked trout, try substituting four ounces of thinly sliced smoked salmon. And of course, as is always the case, buy the best caviar you feel you can afford that day. You, too, will be celebrating with every bite.

1 recipe Pizza Dough (page 100)

2 garlic cloves, minced

2 tablespoons extra-virgin olive oil

$^3/_4$ cup coarsely grated fontina cheese

$^3/_4$ cup coarsely grated mozzarella cheese

$^1/_2$ small red onion, very thinly sliced

6 ounces flaked smoked trout

$^1/_3$ cup crème fraîche

Salt and freshly ground black pepper

1 to 2 tablespoons water

2 tablespoons minced green onions or chives

1 ounce caviar (beluga, sevruga, or osetra) or American sturgeon

Make the pizza dough and let rise.

Thirty minutes before baking, preheat the oven to 500°F. Place a pizza stone on the bottom rack of the oven and heat for at least 30 minutes.

In a bowl, combine the garlic and olive oil and let stand for 30 minutes. In another bowl, combine the fontina and mozzarella and set aside.

Punch down the dough. On a floured surface, divide the dough into 2 pieces and form into balls. Roll 1 piece of dough into a 9-inch circle, $^3/_8$ inch thick. Transfer to a heavily floured pizza peel. Lightly brush the dough to within $^1/_2$ inch of the edge with the garlic oil. Sprinkle half of the cheese mixture over the dough, leaving $^1/_2$ inch around the edge. Spread half of the red onion on top of the cheese. Slide the pizza onto the pizza stone and bake until golden and crisp, 8 to 12 minutes. Remove from the oven.

Distribute half of the trout evenly over the top of the pizza. Season the crème fraîche with salt and pepper and add the water to make an almost pourable consistency. Drizzle half of the crème fraîche lightly over the pizza. Garnish with half each of the green onions and caviar and serve immediately.

Make a second pizza with the remaining ingredients.

Makes two 10- to 11-inch pizzas, to serve 6 as an appetizer or 2 as a main course

TO DRINK: Champagne or sparkling wine

pizza with cherry tomato and basil salad

Whenever I go for pizza, I love to have it with salad. And then I learned about pizzas with salads on top. I call this my "everything-in-one" pizza, because I top crisp, hot, fresh-from-the-oven pizza with a tomato and basil salad. The combination can't be beat. You simply must try this "salad pizza" one time, and, just like me, you'll be hooked.

1 recipe Pizza Dough (page 100)

1½ cups coarsely grated smoked mozzarella cheese (or Scamorza)

2 tablespoons extra-virgin olive oil

2 tablespoons balsamic vinegar

1 garlic clove, minced

Salt and freshly ground black pepper

6 ounces yellow cherry tomatoes, halved

6 ounces red cherry tomatoes, halved

½ cup loosely packed fresh basil leaves, cut into thin strips

Make the pizza dough and let rise.

Thirty minutes before baking, preheat the oven to 500°F. Place a pizza stone on the bottom rack of the oven and heat for at least 30 minutes.

On a floured surface, divide the dough into 2 pieces and form into balls. Roll 1 piece of dough into a 10- to 11-inch circle, ³/₈ inch thick. Transfer to a heavily floured pizza peel. Top with half of the smoked mozzarella cheese, distributing evenly. Slide the pizza onto the pizza stone and bake until golden and crisp, 8 to 12 minutes.

In the meantime, whisk together the oil, vinegar, and garlic in a bowl to make a vinaigrette. Season with salt and pepper. Add the yellow and red cherry tomatoes and toss together.

When the pizza is done, place on a platter. Top with half each of the tomatoes, vinaigrette, and basil. Serve immediately.

Make a second pizza with the remaining ingredients.

Makes two 10- to 11-inch pizzas, to serve 6 as an appetizer or 2 as a main course

TO DRINK: Soave

pizza with arugula and shaved parmigiano

Here is another hot-from-the-oven pizza topped with a cool, refreshing salad—this time arugula dressed with a lemon-garlic vinaigrette and finished with shards of Parmigiano. For variety, add a few paper-thin slices of prosciutto just before serving.

1 recipe Pizza Dough (page 100)
2 garlic cloves, minced
$^1/_4$ cup extra-virgin olive oil
$^3/_4$ cup coarsely grated mozzarella cheese
$^3/_4$ cup coarsely grated fontina cheese
1 tablespoon lemon juice
Salt and freshly ground black pepper
2 large bunches of arugula, ends trimmed
6-ounce piece Parmigiano-Reggiano cheese

Make the pizza dough and let rise.

Thirty minutes before baking, preheat the oven to 500°F. Place a pizza stone on the bottom rack of the oven and heat for at least 30 minutes.

In a bowl, combine half of the garlic and 2 tablespoons of the olive oil and let stand for 30 minutes. In another bowl, combine the mozzarella and fontina and set aside.

For the vinaigrette, whisk together the remaining 2 tablespoons olive oil, the lemon juice, and the remaining garlic in a small bowl. Season to taste with salt and pepper.

Punch down the dough. On a floured surface, divide the dough into 2 pieces and form into balls. Roll 1 piece into a 9-inch circle, $^1/_4$ inch thick. Transfer to a heavily floured pizza peel. Brush the dough to within $^1/_2$ inch of the edge with the garlic-infused oil. Sprinkle half of the cheese mixture over the dough. Slide the pizza onto the pizza stone and bake until golden and crisp, 8 to 10 minutes. Toss the arugula with the vinaigrette and season with salt and pepper. Distribute half on top of the pizza. Shave half of the Parmigiano onto the top and serve immediately.

Make a second pizza with the remaining ingredients.

Makes two 10- to 11-inch pizzas, to serve 6 as an appetizer or 2 as a main course

TO DRINK: Grüner Veltliner, Pinot Grigio, or Sauvignon Blanc

pizza with gorgonzola and tomatoes

I think tomatoes and gorgonzola are a match made in heaven. A few years ago, I visited a little hole-in-the-wall pizza joint that I had heard made the absolute "best of the best" pizza in San Francisco. When I got there, I just couldn't decide which pizza I wanted. I finally ordered this one. When it arrived at my table with the Gorgonzola melting with the tomatoes into the hot crispy dough, I knew it was possible that their other pizzas might taste just as good as that one, but none could have tasted any better.

1 recipe Pizza Dough (page 100)
2 garlic cloves, minced
3 tablespoons extra-virgin olive oil
$^1/_2$ cup coarsely grated fontina cheese
$^1/_2$ cup coarsely grated mozzarella cheese
4 ounces Gorgonzola cheese
12 plum tomatoes (fresh or canned), peeled,
    seeded, and chopped (page 6)
Salt and freshly ground black pepper

Make the pizza dough and let rise.

Thirty minutes before baking, preheat the oven to 500°F. Place a pizza stone on the bottom rack of the oven and heat for at least 30 minutes.

In a small bowl, combine the garlic and 2 tablespoons of the olive oil and let stand for 30 minutes. In another bowl, combine the fontina, mozzarella, and Gorgonzola cheeses and set aside.

In a saucepan over high heat, heat the remaining 1 tablespoon olive oil. Add the tomatoes and bring to a boil. Decrease the heat to low and simmer until the tomatoes are very dry and $^1/_2$ cup remains, 15 to 20 minutes. Season to taste with salt and pepper. Let cool.

Punch down the dough. On a floured surface, divide the dough into 2 pieces and form into balls. Roll 1 piece into a 9-inch circle, $^1/_4$ inch thick. Transfer to a heavily floured pizza peel. Brush the dough to within $^1/_2$ inch of the edge with the garlic-infused oil. Spread half of the tomato sauce on top of the dough to within $^1/_2$ inch of the edge. Sprinkle with half of the cheese. Slide the pizza onto the pizza stone and bake until golden and crisp, 8 to 12 minutes. Remove from the oven and serve immediately.

Make a second pizza with the remaining ingredients.

Makes two 10- 11-inch pizzas, to serve 6 as an appetizer or 2 as a main course

TO DRINK: Dry Riesling or Pinot Noir

calzone with oven-dried tomatoes and roasted peppers

I love dishes like calzones that look as though they're complicated, but are really very easy once you've mastered the dough. The best part is cutting into it at the table to a chorus of "oohs and ahs" as the steam escapes, the cheese oozes out of the center, and the vegetables release their heady aromas. Sometimes, instead of making two large calzones, I will make four individual ones, one per guest. With a green salad, it makes a perfect main course. Note that the tomatoes will need six to seven hours to dry.

1 recipe Calzone Dough (page 100)

3 pounds plum tomatoes, cored and
    halved lenghtwise

Salt

$^1/_4$ cup pitted, coarsely chopped niçoise
    or kalamata olives

2 tablespoons capers, drained

1 red bell pepper, roasted and
    cut into strips (page 6)

$^1/_2$ cup grated fontina cheese

$^1/_2$ cup grated mozzarella cheese

1 cup crumbled goat cheese

2 tablespoons chopped fresh basil

1 tablespoon chopped fresh mint

2 teaspoons chopped fresh oregano

Make the calzone dough and let rise.

To oven-dry the tomatoes, place the tomatoes on a baking sheet, cut side up, and sprinkle with salt. Let sit for 1 hour. Preheat the oven to 250°F. Bake for 5 to 6 hours, until nearly dry. You should have about 1 cup.

Thirty minutes before baking the dough, preheat the oven to 500°F. Place a pizza stone on the bottom rack of the oven and heat for at least 30 minutes.

In a bowl, combine the tomatoes, olives, capers, red bell pepper, fontina, mozzarella, goat cheese, basil, mint, and oregano.

On a floured surface, divide the dough into 2 pieces and form into balls. Roll 1 piece into a 12-inch circle, approximately $^1/_4$ inch thick. Transfer to a heavily floured pizza peel. Spread half of the tomato-cheese mixture on half of the dough, leaving a $1^1/_2$-inch border around the edge. With a pastry brush, moisten the bottom edges of the dough lightly with water and fold the dough over the filling, matching the edges and pressing together well to seal completely. Roll the edges of the dough inward and press to make a tight seal. Slide the calzone onto the pizza stone and bake until golden and crisp, 10 to 12 minutes. Remove from the oven and place on a wooden cutting board. Let rest for 10 minutes before serving.

Make a second calzone with the remaining ingredients.

Makes 2 large or 4 individual-size calzones,
to serve 4 as a main course

TO DRINK: Chianti or Côtes du Rhône

Mains

(continued)

farfalle with olives, capers, tomatoes, and mozzarella

Start by buying the best-quality fresh mozzarella cheese you can afford—preferably buffalo milk mozzarella, if you can find it. Cut it into cubes and, just before serving the hot pasta with tomatoes, add the mozzarella. As you serve the dish, the cheese starts to melt together with the tomatoes. Talk about "melt in your mouth!"

1/4 cup extra-virgin olive oil

6 large tomatoes (about 3 pounds, fresh or canned), peeled, seeded, diced, and drained (page 6)

3 tablespoons capers, drained

3/4 cup assorted imported olives, pitted and coarsely chopped

Salt and freshly ground black pepper

1 pound farfalle pasta

3/4 cup fresh basil leaves

3/4 pound fresh mozzarella cheese, diced

Heat the olive oil in a large skillet over medium-high heat. Add the tomatoes and cook until soft, about 10 minutes. Add the capers and olives and stir together. Season to taste with salt and pepper. Remove the pan from the heat and reserve.

Bring a large pot of salted water to a boil over high heat. Add the pasta and cook until al dente, 10 to 12 minutes. In the meantime, heat the tomato mixture until hot, about 1 minute. Cut the basil into thin strips. When the pasta is done, drain and add the tomato sauce. Stir in the mozzarella and basil and serve immediately.

Serves 6

TO DRINK: Pinot Grigio

spinach and ricotta gnocchi with wilted greens

"Aren't gnocchi those heavy dumplings made with potatoes?" one of my students asked with a frown. I am sure she was remembering poorly made doughy balls that fell to the pit of her stomach with a thud. I reminded her that there are all sorts of gnocchi, but even the potato ones—if made properly—should be light as a cloud, just like these.

2 pounds spinach, stems removed, washed, dried, and chopped

1¼ cups grated Parmigiano-Reggiano cheese

1½ to 2 cups all-purpose flour

1 cup whole-milk ricotta cheese, drained for 2 hours in a cheesecloth-lined sieve

2 large eggs

½ teaspoon freshly grated nutmeg

Salt and freshly ground black pepper

1 cup chicken stock

2 tablespoons extra-virgin olive oil

2 bunches greens (such as Swiss chard, turnip greens, escarole, or beet greens), cut into 1-inch strips

1 teaspoon grated lemon zest

1 garlic clove, minced

Pinch of red pepper flakes

1 tablespoon lemon juice

Place the spinach in a large skillet over medium heat. Cook, tossing constantly, until wilted, about 2 minutes. Remove the spinach from the pan and wring out excess moisture in a clean kitchen towel. Chop and place the spinach in a bowl with ½ cup of the grated Parmigiano, ½ cup of the flour, the ricotta, eggs, nutmeg, and salt and pepper, and mix well. Add additional flour until the mixture is no longer sticky.

Bring a large pot of salted water to a boil over medium-high heat. With a spoon, shape the dough into large, oval, walnut-size balls and roll them in the remaining flour. Place the gnocchi in the water, a few at a time; after they rise to the surface, continue to simmer until firm to the touch, 5 to 10 minutes. Remove with a slotted spoon and place in a well-oiled 2-quart baking dish. Roll the gnocchi to coat them with oil.

Preheat the oven to 400°F.

Pour the chicken stock into a small saucepan. Boil rapidly over high heat until reduced to ½ cup. Set aside.

Heat the olive oil in a large skillet over high heat until hot. Add the greens and toss until the greens wilt, 3 to 4 minutes. Add the lemon zest, garlic, and red pepper flakes. Add the reduced chicken stock and lemon juice and toss until hot, about 30 seconds. Season to taste with salt and pepper.

Ten minutes before serving, place the gnocchi in the oven until warm, about 10 minutes. To serve, place the gnocchi on a serving platter and top with the greens. Sprinkle the top with ¼ cup of the Parmigiano. Pass the remaining ½ cup Parmigiano at the table.

Makes 36 dumplings, to serve 6

TO DRINK: Pinot Blanc or Sauvignon Blanc

fusilli with summer beans and savory

Fresh summer string and shell beans ripen in the garden at the same time. Here, I've combined fresh-from-the-garden shell beans with green or yellow string beans, pasta, and summer savory for a light and fresh-tasting celebration of summer's bounty.

$2^{1}/_{2}$ pounds assorted fresh shell beans
(such as cranberry, lima, scarlet runner,
and black-eyed peas), shelled (about
1 cup)

$1^{1}/_{4}$ pounds assorted string beans (such as
green, yellow, and haricot vert),
trimmed

$2^{1}/_{2}$ cups chicken stock

2 tablespoons extra-virgin olive oil

2 shallots, minced

2 garlic cloves, minced

2 tablespoons chopped fresh flat-leaf parsley

2 tablespoon chopped fresh summer savory

2 teaspoons chopped fresh oregano

Salt and freshly ground black pepper

10 ounces fusilli pasta

Sprigs of summer savory, for garnish

In a large pot of boiling water over high heat, cook the shelled beans until tender, 5 to 10 minutes. Drain and cool. Cut the string beans in half crosswise on the diagonal. In a large pot of boiling salted water over high heat, cook the string beans until tender, 4 to 6 minutes. Drain and cool.

In a saucepan, bring the stock to a boil over medium-high heat and reduce by half. Remove from the heat.

In a large skillet over medium heat, heat the olive oil and cook the shallots until soft, 5 minutes. Add the garlic and stir for 1 minute. Add the shell beans, string beans, parsley, savory, oregano, and the reduced stock. Stir together until warm, about 1 minute. Season with salt and pepper.

Bring a large pot of salted water to a boil over high heat. Add the pasta and cook until the pasta is al dente, 8 to 10 minutes. Drain and toss with the bean mixture. Place in a bowl, garnish with the savory sprigs, and serve.

Serves 6

TO DRINK: Grüner Veltliner

farmer's market risotto with zucchini and their blossoms

When you visit your farmer's market at the crest of summer and find tender young zucchini with their bright yellow flowers still attached, grab them! They're absolutely delicious stuffed, fried, and, most of all, in this zucchini risotto. Stir the blossoms into the almost-finished dish for a splash of color and a bit of peppery flavor. There's a good reason Italians anxiously await their arrival in the markets every year.

1 pound baby zucchini, with blossoms attached

3 cups chicken stock

3 cups water

2 tablespoons extra-virgin olive oil

1 small yellow onion, minced

1 1/2 cups Arborio, Vialone Nano, or Carnaroli rice

1/2 cup dry white wine, such as Sauvignon Blanc

Salt and freshly ground black pepper

2 tablespoons chopped fresh flat-leaf parsley

2 tablespoons unsalted butter, at room temperature

1 cup finely grated Parmigiano-Reggiano cheese

Remove the flowers from the zucchini and slice the zucchini crosswise into 1/4-inch slices. Cut the blossoms into thirds crosswise.

In a saucepan, combine the chicken stock and water and bring to a boil over high heat. Decrease the heat to low and maintain just below the boiling point on a back burner of the stove.

Heat the olive oil in a large, heavy skillet over medium heat. Add the onion and cook until soft, about 7 minutes. Add the zucchini and cook for 1 minute. Add the rice and stir to coat the rice with oil until the edges of the rice are translucent and there is a white dot in the center of each grain, about 3 minutes. Add the wine and cook, stirring, until the wine evaporates, about 1 minute. Add 1/4 teaspoon of salt and about 1 cup of the stock and stir the rice constantly to wipe it away from the bottom and sides of the pot. When most of the liquid has been absorbed, but the rice is still loose, add another ladleful of stock and continue to cook the risotto. Continue to add stock a ladle at a time, stirring constantly, until the rice is just beyond the chalky stage, 18 to 22 minutes. If you run out of stock, add hot water.

Remove from the stove and stir in another ladleful of stock, the parsley, butter, zucchini blossoms, and 1/2 cup of the Parmigiano. Season to taste with salt and pepper. Cover and let sit off the heat for 5 minutes.

To serve, remove the cover, stir, sprinkle with the remaining 1/2 cup Parmigiano, and serve immediately.

Serves 6

TO DRINK: White Rhône blend

linguine with goat cheese and arugula

Chèvre is French for "goat," but in the United States, the word *chèvre* means goat cheese and, remarkably, it's now made in nearly all fifty states. Tart and tangy goat cheese makes a luscious creamy sauce for pasta tossed with spicy pancetta, garlic, red pepper flakes, and fresh, peppery arugula. Be careful, though—you'll be making this easy and addictive dish very often!

$^1/_4$ cup extra-virgin olive oil

5 ounces pancetta, diced

1 garlic clove, minced

$^1/_2$ cup heavy cream

8 ounces fresh goat cheese

$^1/_4$ cup snipped fresh chives

$^1/_4$ teaspoon red pepper flakes

Salt and freshly ground black pepper

12 ounces linguine pasta

$1^1/_4$ cups grated Parmigiano-Reggiano cheese

4 cups arugula, stems removed and very coarsely chopped

Warm the olive oil in a large skillet over medium-low heat. Add the pancetta and cook until light golden, 10 to 15 minutes. Remove the mixture from the pan, place in a bowl, and let cool. Add the garlic, heavy cream, goat cheese, chives, and red pepper flakes and mash together. Season to taste with salt and pepper. Set aside.

Bring a large pot of salted water to a boil over high heat. Add the pasta and cook until al dente, 7 to 9 minutes. Drain the pasta, reserving 2 tablespoons of pasta water. Toss the hot pasta, pasta water, and half the Parmigiano with the goat cheese mixture. Coat the pasta well with the sauce. Add the arugula and toss together. Place on a platter, garnish with the remaining half of the Parmigiano, and serve immediately.

Serves 6

TO DRINK: Sauvignon Blanc

penne with olio santo, ricotta salata, olives, and mint

In Italy, *olio santo* (saint's oil) is a favorite condiment that is made with spicy hot dried red peppers added with abandon to fruity extra-virgin olive oil. Olio santo is drizzled onto a finished dish just before serving to give a bit of extra zing to almost anything. It certainly does the trick here when combined with pasta, salty ricotta salata, briney black olives, and cool mint. Note that you'll need to prepare the olio santo two hours in advance.

1/4 cup extra-virgin olive oil

1/2 teaspoon red pepper flakes or
    2 dried hot red chiles, crumbled

2 cups chicken stock

12 ounces penne or fusilli pasta

1/2 pound ricotta salata cheese, crumbled

3/4 cup imported black olives, pitted and
    coarsely chopped

Salt and freshly ground black pepper

3 tablespoons chopped fresh mint,
    for garnish

To make olio santo, heat the olive oil in a saucepan over medium heat until warm. Add the red pepper flakes, remove from the heat immediately, and let sit for 2 hours. Strain and discard the pepper.

In the meantime, bring the chicken stock to a boil over medium-high heat and reduce until 3/4 cup remains. Reserve.

Bring a large pot of salted water to a boil over high heat. Add the pasta and cook until al dente, 8 to 10 minutes. Drain and immediately return to the pot. Add the reduced chicken stock, olio santo, ricotta salata, and olives. Toss together and season to taste with salt and pepper. Place in a serving bowl and sprinkle with the mint. Serve immediately.

Serves 6

TO DRINK: Dolcetto

fettuccine with tomatoes, basil, and crisp bread crumbs

If there was ever a food marriage blessed by the gods, it's surely tomatoes and basil. Pick vine-ripened tomatoes at their height of sweetness, combine them with tender leaves of young basil and pasta, and top the whole dish with crunchy golden bread crumbs. This is what summer should be, when the best peak-of-season ingredients stand by themselves and make the finished dish shine.

1 cup very coarse fresh bread crumbs, for garnish

6 tablespoons extra-virgin olive oil

Salt and freshly ground black pepper

3^1/$_2$ tablespoons balsamic vinegar

2 cups yellow cherry tomatoes, halved

2 cups red cherry tomatoes, halved

12 ounces fettuccine pasta

^{1}/$_2$ cup fresh basil leaves, cut into thin strips, for garnish

Preheat the oven to 375°F.

Place the bread crumbs on a baking sheet. Drizzle with 2 tablespoons of the olive oil and toss the bread crumbs to distribute the oil evenly. Season the bread crumbs with salt and pepper. Bake in the middle of the oven, tossing occasionally, until they turn golden brown, 8 to 10 minutes. Remove from the oven and let cool.

In a bowl, whisk together the remaining 4 tablespoons olive oil and the balsamic vinegar to make a vinaigrette. Season to taste with salt and pepper. Add the tomatoes and stir together. Set aside.

Fill a large pot three-quarters full with salted water and bring to a boil over high heat. Add the pasta and cook until al dente, 10 to 12 minutes.

Drain the pasta and toss with the tomatoes and vinaigrette. Place in a serving bowl and garnish with the basil and bread crumbs. Serve immediately.

Serves 6

TO DRINK: Pinot Grigio

italian "mac and cheese"

I am not joking—this dish is dangerous and should come with a warning. Imagine whole wheat penne pasta mixed with a béchamel sauce made with three cheeses and then the whole thing baked in the oven. It's easy to make, and the results defy the amount of work it takes to get there. I warned you—this stuff is sinful.

2 tablespoons unsalted butter

$1/4$ cup all-purpose flour

$2^3/4$ cups whole milk

1 cup grated fontina cheese

5 ounces Gorgonzola cheese

$3/4$ cup grated Parmigiano-Reggiano cheese

Salt and freshly ground black pepper

$1/2$ pound whole wheat penne pasta

$1/3$ cup fresh bread crumbs

In a saucepan, heat the butter over medium heat. Add the flour and, with a whisk, stir until bubbling, 2 minutes. Add the milk and whisk together. With a wooden spoon, stir until the mixture thickens. Add the fontina, Gorgonzola, and Parmigiano and stir until the cheese melts. Season with salt and pepper. Remove from the heat and set aside.

Preheat the oven to 375°F.

Bring a large pot of salted water to a boil over high heat. Add the pasta and cook until al dente, 10 to 12 minutes. Drain and toss with the sauce. Transfer the pasta and sauce to a lightly oiled 2-quart baking dish. Sprinkle with the bread crumbs. Bake in the oven until the top is golden and the sauce is bubbling, 25 to 30 minutes. Serve hot.

Serves 6

TO DRINK: Chianti or Grenache Blanc

lasagne with wild mushrooms, leeks, and gorgonzola

My mother has always had the knack for making great lasagne. She definitely perfected the traditional version comprising tomato sauce, mozzarella, and ricotta. Here, I have replaced the tomatoes with wild mushrooms, leeks, and a creamy béchamel made with Gorgonzola. If wild mushrooms are unavailable, use whichever cultivated mushrooms look best.

$1/2$ pound dried lasagne noodles

15 ounces ricotta cheese

$3/4$ cup grated Parmigiano-Reggiano cheese

Salt and freshly ground black pepper

$1/4$ cup extra-virgin olive oil

5 large leeks, white plus 3 inches of the green part, cut into 1-inch dice

$1 1/2$ pounds wild mushrooms, thinly sliced

5 garlic cloves, minced

$1/4$ cup ($1/2$ stick) unsalted butter

$4 1/2$ tablespoons all-purpose flour

$3 1/2$ cups whole milk

6 ounces Gorgonzola, Stilton, or Roquefort cheese

Freshly grated nutmeg

4 ounces whole-milk mozzarella cheese, coarsely grated

Bring a large pot of salted water to a boil over high heat. Add the lasagne noodles and cook until al dente, 8 to 12 minutes. While the pasta is cooking, fill a large bowl with cold water. When the pasta is done, drain the pasta and place in the bowl of water to cool. After 5 minutes, drain the pasta and place the pieces in a single layer on a baking sheet. Cover with plastic wrap and set aside.

In a small bowl, mix together the ricotta and Parmigiano, and season with salt and pepper. Set aside.

Heat 2 tablespoons of the olive oil in a skillet over medium-low heat. Add the leeks and cook, uncovered, stirring occasionally, until the leeks are very soft and light golden, about 30 minutes. Remove the leeks from the pan and reserve.

Heat the remaining 2 tablespoons olive oil in a large skillet. Add the mushrooms and cook until they are soft and the liquid has evaporated, 7 to 10 minutes. Add the garlic and stir for 1 minute. Add to the leeks and stir together.

Melt the butter in a saucepan over medium-high heat. Stir in the flour and cook, uncovered, stirring constantly, for 2 to 3 minutes. Add the milk and whisk constantly until it comes to a boil and thickens, 4 to 5 minutes. Add the Gorgonzola and stir until smooth. Season with salt, pepper, and nutmeg.

Preheat the oven to 375°F. Oil a 13 by 9-inch baking dish. Cover the bottom of the baking dish with a single layer of pasta. Cover the pasta with one-third of the ricotta mixture. Sprinkle one-third of the mushroom-leek mixture over the ricotta. Spread one-third of the cheese sauce over the vegetables. Repeat with the remaining 2 layers. Sprinkle the mozzarella evenly over the top layer. Bake on the top rack of the oven until the surface is golden and bubbling around the edges, 40 to 50 minutes. Remove from the oven and let stand 15 minutes before serving.

Serves 8 to 10

TO DRINK: Red Burgundy or Rioja

egg pasta dough

I learned this pasta recipe from an Italian friend, Gionanna, when I was teaching in the Veneto. I love it because it's so easy and foolproof. The only thing you need to watch out for is the amount of liquid you add to the food processor. Add enough so that the texture of the dough is crumbly and hasn't formed a ball yet. If it forms a ball, it will be too wet. I use this recipe for just about every pasta application.

2 cups all-purpose flour

$^1/_4$ teaspoon salt

2 large eggs

2 tablespoons water

In the bowl of a food processor, pulse together the flour and salt. Add the eggs and water and process until the dough forms a soft ball, but is not sticky. If it is sticky, add more flour, 1 tablespoon at a time, until it isn't sticky. If it is dry, add additional water, 1 tablespoon at a time. Remove the dough from the food processor bowl and knead on a very lightly floured board until soft and smooth, 2 to 3 minutes. Wrap the dough in plastic wrap and place in the refrigerator for 30 minutes or up to 1 day to rest before using.

Makes approximately 1 pound pasta

homemade ricotta-and-mint ravioli with sweet tomatoes

Ravioli takes some effort, but once you have mastered the technique (practice makes perfect) you'll be eager to make these again and again. These are light and flavorfully satisfying, made with ricotta, mint, and tomato, and they can even be made in advance and frozen. When you have the urge for ravioli, pop these beauties right out of the freezer directly into boiling water.

1 recipe Egg Pasta Dough (opposite page)

1 pound fresh spinach, washed and dried

3 ounces mascarpone cheese

3 ounces ricotta cheese

1 cup grated Parmigiano-Reggiano cheese

1 large egg yolk

1 small garlic clove, minced

1 tablespoon chopped fresh mint

Salt and freshly ground black pepper

Large pinch of freshly grated nutmeg

3 tablespoons extra-virgin olive oil

5 garlic cloves, bruised

4 cups peeled, seeded, and chopped tomatoes (fresh or canned) (page 6)

$1/3$ cup fresh basil leaves, for garnish

Prepare the pasta dough.

Heat a large skillet over medium heat. Wilt the spinach, tossing continuously. Place the spinach on paper towels and press to remove all moisture. Chop the spinach and place in a large bowl. Add the mascarpone, ricotta, $1/3$ cup of the Parmigiano, egg yolk, minced garlic, and mint, and mix well. Season to taste with salt, pepper, and nutmeg. Place in the refrigerator until needed.

Divide the dough into 4 pieces. By machine or by hand, roll the pasta $1/8$ inch thick. Place a pasta sheet on a lightly floured work surface. Using a tablespoon, place spoonfuls of the cheese in mounds onto the sheet just below the center, spacing them about 2 inches apart. With a spray mister filled with water, lightly mist around the mounds of filling. Fold the top of the pasta over the filling, matching the edges. Press around the filling and the edges to seal the ravioli. Using a fluted cutting wheel, cut along the long edge, close to the edge. Discard the scraps. Cut between the filling. Place them in a single layer on a well-floured baking sheet. Repeat with the remaining 3 pieces of pasta and filling.

Heat the olive oil in a large skillet over medium-high heat. Add the 5 bruised garlic cloves and cook until golden, 2 to 3 minutes. Remove and discard them. Add the tomatoes to the pan and let cook until the tomatoes are soft, 5 to 10 minutes. Season to taste with salt and pepper, and cook until half of the liquid has evaporated, about 10 minutes.

Bring a large pot of salted water to a boil over high heat. Add the ravioli and cook until al dente, 3 to 4 minutes. Drain and place in a bowl. Add the tomato sauce and gently mix together. Place on a platter and sprinkle with the remaining $2/3$ cup Parmigiano and the basil leaves.

Makes about 32 large ravioli, to serve 6

TO DRINK: Chianti

linguine with spicy hot crab and tomatoes

Dungeness crab is one of the greatest gifts from the sea. Combine its sweetness with summer tomatoes and basil, and just the right amount of red pepper flakes to leave you with a hint of heat in the back of your throat. I could eat this dish all day long.

2 cooked Dungeness or blue crabs
(1 to 1^1/$_2$ pounds each)

^{1}/$_4$ cup extra-virgin olive oil

5 garlic cloves, crushed

1^1/$_2$ cups dry red wine, such as
Cabernet Sauvignon

5 cups peeled, seeded, and chopped tomatoes
(fresh or canned) (page 6)

2 cups bottled clam juice or fish stock

3 tablespoons red wine vinegar

32 fresh basil leaves, 12 torn into small
pieces, and 20 cut into thin strips,
for garnish

1 teaspoon chopped fresh oregano
or marjoram

1^1/$_4$ teaspoons red pepper flakes

Salt

1 pound dried linguine pasta

Clean and crack the crab, or have your fishmonger do it. Cut the claws and bodies into several pieces.

In a saucepan, heat the olive oil over medium-low heat. Add the garlic and cook until soft, but not golden, about 1 minute. Remove the garlic and discard. Add the wine, increase the heat to high, and simmer until it has reduced by three-quarters, 5 to 7 minutes. Using a food mill, puree the tomatoes directly into the pan. Add the clam juice, vinegar, torn basil pieces, oregano, red pepper flakes, and salt to taste. As soon as the mixture comes to a boil, decrease the heat to medium-low, and simmer until slightly thickened, 8 to 10 minutes. Add the crab and continue to cook for 5 minutes. Taste and season with salt.

Bring a large pot of salted water to a boil over high heat. Add the pasta and cook until al dente, 5 to 8 minutes. Drain and toss with the crab and tomato sauce. Serve immediately, garnished with the strips of basil.

Serves 6

TO DRINK: Vouvray

risotto with lemon shrimp

A dish of lemon, shrimp, and rice is an ancient food combination in a multitude of world cuisines, probably because it tastes so good. Making good risotto requires a little time and patience, and a bit of muscle. Making great risotto requires a little trick I'd love to share: Just when the risotto goes beyond the chalky stage, remove the pan from the heat, and in this case, add a ladleful of broth, a bit of butter, the cooked shrimp, lemon zest, lemon juice, and the Parmigiano, and let it sit, tightly covered, off the heat for 5 minutes. Give it a stir and you have the creamiest risotto. *Perfetto!*

$1^{1}/_{2}$ pounds medium-size shrimp, peeled, deveined, and shells reserved

2 cups bottled clam juice

3 cups water

$1^{1}/_{4}$ cups dry white wine, such as Sauvignon Blanc

$^{1}/_{4}$ cup extra-virgin olive oil

1 medium-size onion, chopped

2 cups Arborio, Vialone Nano, or Carnaroli rice

3 tablespoons lemon juice

2 tablespoons unsalted butter

$^{3}/_{4}$ cup grated Parmigiano-Reggiano cheese

$1^{1}/_{2}$ teaspoons grated lemon zest

Salt and freshly ground black pepper

Whole leaves of fresh flat-leaf parsley, for garnish

Place the shrimp shells, clam juice, water, and $^{1}/_{2}$ cup of the wine in a saucepan. Bring to a boil over high heat. Decrease the heat to low, cover, and simmer slowly for 15 minutes. Strain the shrimp stock and place in a saucepan on the back burner of the stove, adjusting the heat to maintain just below a simmer.

In a large heavy saucepan over medium-high heat, warm 2 tablespoons of the olive oil. Add the shrimp and cook until they curl slightly, about 2 minutes. Add $^{1}/_{4}$ cup of the wine and reduce by half. Remove the mixture from the pan and reserve.

Add the remaining 2 tablespoons olive oil to the pan. Add the onion and cook until soft, about 7 minutes. Add the rice and stir to coat the grains with oil, about 3 minutes. Add the remaining $^{1}/_{2}$ cup wine and $1^{1}/_{2}$ tablespoons of the lemon juice and cook, stirring, until the liquid evaporates, about 1 minute. Add about 1 cup of warm shrimp stock, stirring the rice constantly. When most of the liquid has been absorbed, add another ladleful of stock and continue to cook until the rice is just beyond the chalky stage, 18 to 22 minutes. If you run out of stock, use hot water.

Remove the pan from the heat, add the shrimp, a ladleful of stock, the butter, half the Parmigiano, the lemon zest, and the remaining $1^{1}/_{2}$ tablespoons lemon juice. Season to taste with salt and pepper. Cover and let stand for 5 minutes. Remove the cover and stir. Place in serving bowls, sprinkle with the remaining half of the Parmigiano, garnish with parsley, and serve immediately.

Serves 6

TO DRINK: White Burgundy or Chablis

seared scallops with watercress and lemon relish

This dish is proof positive that simple pleasures truly are the best. Sear some really fresh sweet sea scallops and place them in the center of the plate. Top them with a lemon relish made with extra-virgin olive oil, lemon zest, parsley, shallots, and lemon juice, and, finally, top with a watercress salad. Simple, yes, but so full of bright, fresh flavors—the essence of wine country cooking.

6 tablespoons extra-virgin olive oil

2 teaspoons grated lemon zest

2 tablespoons chopped fresh flat-leaf parsley

2 shallots, minced

2 tablespoons lemon juice

Salt and freshly ground black pepper

1 1/2 pounds sea scallops

1 bunch of watercress, stems removed, for garnish

Lemon wedges, for garnish

In a small bowl, whisk together 4 tablespoons of the olive oil, the lemon zest, parsley, shallots, and lemon juice to make a relish. Season to taste with salt and pepper.

Remove the muscle from the side of each scallop and discard. In a large skillet over medium high heat, warm the remaining 2 tablespoons olive oil. Add the scallops in a single layer. Do not over-crowd the pan. Cook the scallops until golden on 1 side, about 2 minutes. Turn the scallops, season with salt and pepper, and continue to cook until the scallops are golden and slightly firm to the touch, 2 to 3 minutes.

To serve, divide the scallops among 6 serving plates. Spoon the relish over the scallops, distributing evenly. Top with the watercress, garnish with lemon wedges, and serve immediately.

Serves 6

TO DRINK: Grüner Veltliner

shellfish stew with orzo

Any kind of manipulation, culinary trick, or complicated technique is lost on me. The simplest dishes with the most "wow" factor are always preferable. So get ready for a great one! It starts with the very freshest shellfish you can find—clams, mussels, scallops, and shrimp—in a tomato broth spiked with garlic, red pepper flakes, and white wine. Add some orzo, the quick-cooking, rice-shaped Italian pasta, and it it's a soup, it's a stew, it's a tasty meal in a bowl.

3 cups bottled clam juice or fish stock

1 pound clams

1 pound mussels

1/2 pound scallops

1/2 pound medium-size shrimp, peeled and deveined

3 tablespoons extra-virgin olive oil

1 small yellow onion, minced

3 garlic cloves, minced

Small pinch of red pepper flakes

1 cup dry white wine, such as Sauvignon Blanc

1 1/2 cups water

2 bay leaves

1 1/2 cups peeled, seeded, and chopped tomatoes (fresh or canned) (page 6)

1 teaspoon red wine vinegar

1 cup orzo pasta

3 tablespoons chopped fresh flat-leaf parsley

Large pinch of saffron threads

Salt and freshly ground black pepper

Bring the clam juice to a boil in a large soup pot over medium-high heat. Add the clams, cover, and cook until the shells open, 3 to 4 minutes. As the clams open, remove them from the pan with tongs and place them in a large bowl. Discard any that have not opened. Repeat with the mussels, cooking for 2 to 3 minutes. Remove and discard top and bottom shells from half of the clams and the mussels, retaining all the meat and keeping the shellfish in the shell in the same bowl as the de-shelled meat. Reserve the broth. Remove the muscle from the side of each scallop. Add the raw scallops and shrimp to the bowl with the cooked shellfish. Reserve.

Heat the olive oil in the soup pot over medium-low heat. Add the onion and sauté until soft, about 7 minutes. Add the garlic and red pepper flakes and sauté for 1 minute. Increase the heat to high and immediately add the wine. Reduce by half, about 2 minutes. Add the water, bay leaves, tomatoes, vinegar, and reserved broth, and bring to a boil over medium-high heat. Decrease the heat to low, add the orzo, cover, and simmer for 2 minutes. Add the parsley, saffron, and shellfish to the soup pot and simmer for 2 minutes. Turn off the heat and let sit for 3 minutes. Season to taste with salt and pepper.

Ladle the soup into bowls, distributing the shellfish evenly, and serve immediately.

Serves 6

TO DRINK: Chianti, Barbera, Dolcetto, or Pinot Noir

shellfish cakes with lime tartar sauce

Why is it that whenever people see crab cakes, shrimp cakes, or shellfish cakes on a menu, they order them? I know I love them and always order them. Lately, though, I have been making them at home. They are so simple, and then you can eat as many as you like. I have been using this recipe for years and everyone loves it.

1¼ cups prepared or homemade mayonnaise (page 87, omit lemons and water to thin)

1 teaspoon Dijon mustard

1 teaspoon grated lime zest

1 tablespoon lime juice

¼ cup minced cornichons (gherkins)

Salt and freshly ground black pepper

2 tablespoons unsalted butter

1 bunch of green onions, white and green parts, thinly sliced

¾ cup chopped celery

1 cup crushed saltine crackers

1 tablespoon dry mustard

1 teaspoon hot pepper sauce, such as Tabasco

2 teaspoons Worcestershire sauce

2 large eggs, well beaten

3 tablespoons finely chopped flat-leaf parsley

6 ounces cooked crabmeat

6 ounces cooked shrimp, peeled and chopped

6 ounces cooked scallops, chopped

2 cups fresh bread crumbs

¼ cup vegetable oil or melted unsalted butter

For the tartar sauce, combine 1 cup of the mayonnaise, the mustard, lime zest, lime juice, and cornichons in a bowl and mix well. Season to taste with salt and pepper. Set aside.

Melt the butter in a large skillet and cook the green onions and celery slowly, over low heat, in a covered pan, stirring occasionally, until they are soft, about 12 minutes. Drain and cool. Add the saltines, dry mustard, hot pepper sauce, Worcestershire, eggs, remaining ¼ cup mayonnaise, parsley, crabmeat, shrimp, and scallops, and season with salt and pepper. Mix well. If the mixture is wet, add enough bread crumbs to absorb the moisture so they hold their shape. Shape the batter into 2½-inch cakes. Dredge them lightly in the bread crumbs.

Heat 2 tablespoons of the vegetable oil in a skillet over medium heat. Sauté half of the shellfish cakes in a single layer, 3 minutes per side, until golden brown. Drain on paper towels. Repeat with the remaining oil and shellfish cakes. Serve immediately with the tartar sauce.

Serves 6

TO DRINK: Sparkling wine

grilled swordfish skewers
with olive "caviar"

Cooking has always been my greatest passion, but I'm not one to spend hours and hours laboring over a dish or recipe. Instead, I tend toward simple-to-prepare dishes with lots of flavor, focusing on the finest fresh ingredients. That's what this dish is all about. Thread some chunks of swordfish onto skewers, grill them over a hot fire, and serve them with a relish made with green and black olives, garlic, parsley, and a splash of white wine vinegar. Sometimes, I'll add a handful of toasted chopped almonds for a little crunch.

2 lemons

1/2 cup extra-virgin olive oil

2 garlic cloves, crushed

Salt and freshly ground black pepper

1 1/2 pounds fresh swordfish, cut into
    1-inch chunks

12 bamboo skewers

2 anchovy fillets, boned, soaked in cold
    water for 10 minutes, patted dry,
    and minced

1/3 cup imported green olives (such as
    picholine), pitted and chopped

1/3 cup imported black olives (such as
    kalamata or niçoise), chopped

1/3 cup Spanish green olives with
    pimiento, chopped

1 garlic clove, minced

1/2 cup chopped fresh flat-leaf parsley,
    plus some whole leaves, for garnish

1 tablespoon white wine vinegar

6 lemon wedges, for garnish

With a vegetable peeler, peel the lemon zest into long strips, avoiding the pith. In a large dish, combine the strips of lemon peel, 2 tablespoons of the olive oil, and the crushed garlic, and season with salt and pepper. Add the swordfish chunks, toss to coat, cover, and refrigerate for 2 hours.

Juice the lemons and soak the bamboo skewers in half of the lemon juice for 1 hour. Reserve the remaining juice.

Heat a charcoal grill.

In a small bowl, combine the anchovies, olives, garlic, parsley, vinegar, the reserved lemon juice, and the remaining 6 tablespoons olive oil to make a relish. Season to taste with salt and pepper.

Skewer the swordfish. Grill the skewers, turning every 2 minutes, until cooked but still slightly pink inside, about 6 to 7 minutes total.

Remove the swordfish skewers from the grill and place on a platter. Spoon the relish over the skewers and garnish with the lemon wedges and parsley.

Serves 6

TO DRINK: Light red Syrah or rosé

grilled sea bass with almond romesco

When I see freshly caught fish at my favorite fishmonger, I immediately want to grill it over mesquite charcoal on my outdoor grill. Hot from the embers, the skin is crisp and the juicy flesh falls from the bone. Serve it with a Spanish-inspired romesco sauce, made with tomatoes, almonds, hazelnuts, hot and sweet peppers, and garlic. You can make the sauce earlier in the day, if needed.

3 medium-size ripe red tomatoes

4 garlic cloves, unpeeled

2 dried chiles, such as anchos

$1/4$ teaspoon red pepper flakes

$1/2$ cup water

5 tablespoons red wine vinegar

$1/4$ cup extra-virgin olive oil,
   plus more for brushing

1 slice coarse-textured country-style
   white bread

12 almonds, skins removed

12 hazelnuts, skins removed

$3/4$ teaspoon sweet paprika

Salt and freshly ground black pepper

2 whole striped bass or other firm white fish
   ($1^{1}/2$ to $1^{3}/4$ pounds each), gutted and
   scaled, or 6 fillets (6 to 8 ounces each)

Sprigs of fresh flat-leaf parsley, for garnish

Preheat the oven to 350°F. Place the tomatoes and garlic in a roasting pan and bake for about 30 minutes. Remove from the oven and peel, core, and seed the tomatoes. Peel the garlic and reserve both.

Place the dried chiles and red pepper flakes in a saucepan with the water and 3 tablespoons of the vinegar. Bring to a boil over high heat, decrease the heat to low, cover, and simmer slowly for 10 minutes. Turn off the heat and let steep for 30 minutes.

Strain the chiles, discard the seeds and liquid, and finely chop them.

To make the romescu sauce, heat 1 tablespoon of the oil in a small skillet over medium heat and fry the bread until golden. Transfer to a food processor. Add another 1 tablespoon oil to the pan and fry the almonds and hazelnuts until golden, 1 to 2 minutes. Add the nuts to the processor along with the tomatoes, garlic, chiles, and paprika. With the motor running, gradually pour in the remaining 2 tablespoons olive oil and the remaining 2 tablespoons vinegar, and season with salt and pepper; puree until smooth. Strain through a coarse mesh strainer. Let sit at room temperature for 1 hour.

Preheat an outdoor grill. Wash the fish and pat dry. Brush the fish lightly with oil. Grill the fish, 4 inches from the coals, until golden on 1 side, 6 to 7 minutes. Turn the fish and continue to cook until golden and cooked, 6 to 7 minutes. The fish is done when the thickest part reaches 140°F.

To serve, place the fish on a platter and spoon the sauce over the top. Garnish with the whole sprigs of parsley and serve immediately.

Serves 6

TO DRINK: Verdejo

tuna with tomatoes, capers, and basil

This recipe calls for a big chunk of fresh tuna, 3 to 4 inches thick. You may have to order it from your fishmonger a day in advance. Dredge the tuna in seasoned flour, brown it, and braise it in white wine and tomatoes, similar to braising meat, but of course, it cooks in a fraction of the time. With the addition of red onions, garlic, red pepper flakes, capers, and basil, the flavors are unbeatable. The finished tuna resembles very tender red meat with delicate flavors.

1 cup all-purpose flour

Salt and freshly ground black pepper

2 pounds tuna loin in 1 piece,
    at least 3 to 4 inches thick

$1/4$ cup extra-virgin olive oil

1 large red onion, cut into large chunks

4 garlic cloves, thinly sliced

1 cup dry white wine

3 cups peeled, seeded, and coarsely chopped
    tomatoes (fresh or canned) (page 6)

1 cup bottled clam juice or fish stock

$1/8$ teaspoon red pepper flakes

$1/4$ cup capers, drained

$1/2$ cup torn fresh basil leaves

Spread the flour on a large plate. Season with salt and pepper. Dredge the tuna in the flour so that it is coated on all sides. Tap off the excess flour. Warm 2 tablespoons of the olive oil in a large, heavy soup pot over medium-high heat. Add the tuna and sear, turning occasionally, until a golden brown crust forms on all sides, 2 minutes on each side. Transfer the tuna to a platter and cover with aluminum foil to keep warm. Wipe out the pot.

Add the remaining 2 tablespoons olive oil to the pot and heat over medium heat. Add the onion and cook until soft, 10 minutes. Add the garlic and

cook, stirring, for 30 seconds. Increase the heat to high, add the wine, bring to a boil, and reduce by half, 2 to 3 minutes. Add the tomatoes, clam juice, and red pepper flakes and bring to a boil. Decrease the heat to low and simmer until it is reduced by half, 5 to 10 minutes. Add the capers and season with salt and pepper.

Return the tuna to the pot, cover, and cook slowly, turning and basting occasionally, until the tuna is medium-rare. To test for doneness, insert a small paring knife into the center of the tuna and hold it there for 1 or 2 seconds. Remove the knife and test the warmth of the blade against the inside of your wrist. It should be warm. Transfer the tuna to a platter and cover with foil again.

To serve, add the basil to the sauce and stir together. To finish the sauce, if the flavor is thin, simmer to reduce and concentrate the flavors. If the sauce is too thick, add additional clam juice or water. Slice the tuna into thick slices and spoon the sauce and vegetables over the tuna. Serve immediately.

Serves 6

TO DRINK: Rosé

crisp salmon with green herb and caper sauce

This technique for cooking salmon is triple F—fast, fantastic, and foolproof. All you need is a non-stick pan, a thin film of olive oil on the bottom of the pan, high heat, and a few fillets of freshly caught, skinless wild salmon. When cooked, the outside of the fish is crisp and golden, while the inside is juicy and tender. Serve it with a green herb and caper sauce, also known as *salsa verde* in Italy. By the way, this versatile sauce is good with just about any kind of meat, poultry, or fish.

$^1/_2$ cup chopped fresh flat-leaf parsley

3 tablespoons chopped fresh chives

$^1/_2$ teaspoon chopped fresh thyme

$^1/_2$ teaspoon chopped fresh oregano

$^1/_4$ teaspoon chopped fresh rosemary

$^1/_4$ teaspoon chopped fresh sage

3 tablespoons capers, drained and chopped

2 garlic cloves, minced

$^1/_2$ cup extra-virgin olive oil

Salt and freshly ground black pepper

6 salmon fillets (about 2 pounds total),
    skin removed

3 tablespoons lemon juice

6 lemon wedges, for garnish

In a bowl, stir together the parsley, chives, thyme, oregano, rosemary, sage, capers, garlic, and 6 tablespoons of the olive oil. Season to taste with salt and pepper.

Heat the remaining 2 tablespoons olive oil over high heat in a large nonstick pan. Add the salmon in a single layer and cook until golden and crisp on 1 side, about 3 minutes. Turn the salmon carefully, season with salt and pepper, and continue to cook until golden and crisp on the second side, 2 to 3 minutes.

In the meantime, add the lemon juice to the herb-caper sauce. To serve, place 1 salmon fillet on each plate and top with the sauce. Garnish with lemon wedges and serve immediately.

Serves 6

TO DRINK: Sauvignon Blanc or Spanish Cava

salmon with asparagus and blood oranges

You know my mantra—fresh, seasonal, and simple. Celebrate the seasons. In this case, let it be spring, when citrus and asparagus are at their peak. Combine them with a piece of wild salmon and the flavors sing. If blood oranges are unavailable, substitute navel oranges.

1 navel orange

1 teaspoon grated fresh ginger

2 tablespoons balsamic vinegar

1 tablespoon white wine vinegar

3 tablespoons extra-virgin olive oil, plus more for brushing

Salt and freshly ground black pepper

3 blood oranges

1½ pounds asparagus, ends trimmed and cut into 2-inch pieces

6 salmon fillets (6 ounces each)

Grate the peel of the navel orange to make 1 teaspoon zest. Place the zest in a small bowl. Juice the navel orange and add it to the zest along with the ginger, balsamic vinegar, white wine vinegar, and 3 tablespoons olive oil to make a vinaigrette. Season to taste with salt and pepper and set aside.

Cut off the tops and bottoms of the blood oranges. With a knife, remove all of the peel so that no white pith remains. Cut the oranges crosswise into ¼-inch slices. Remove any seeds and reserve.

Bring a large saucepan of salted water to a boil over medium-high heat. Add the asparagus and cook until tender, yet crisp, 3 to 4 minutes.

Lightly brush the salmon with oil. Heat a ridged grill over medium-high heat for about 5 minutes.

Grill the salmon, skin side down, until golden and crisp, 3 to 4 minutes. Turn the salmon, season with salt and pepper, and continue to cook until done, 2 to 3 minutes more.

To serve, place 1 piece of salmon in the middle of each plate. Place the asparagus and orange slices around the salmon. Drizzle the vinaigrette over the salmon, asparagus, and oranges, distributing evenly, and serve immediately.

Serves 6

TO DRINK: Albarino

oyster, fennel, and leek stew

It's very seldom that we get snow in the wine country, but we do have rainstorms, and for us, the rains signify winter. These are the kinds of nights that beg for soups and stews. This particular stew is made with fennel, leeks, celery, and potatoes. I puree a bit of the mixture at the end and add it back into the stew to give it a rich texture without all the calories. Just before serving, I poach fresh oysters in the stew. This is a dinner to enjoy in front of a cozy fire.

2 dozen fresh oysters, in their shells

3 tablespoons unsalted butter

1 medium-size yellow onion, cut into
   $^1/_2$-inch dice

5 large leeks, white and 2 inches of
   green part, cut into $^1/_2$-inch slices

4 celery stalks, cut into $^1/_2$-inch slices,
   leaves reserved for garnish

2 fennel bulbs, cut into $^1/_2$-inch dice,
   tops chopped and reserved for garnish

3 cups bottled clam juice or fish stock

2 cups water

$1^1/_2$ pounds potatoes, peeled and
   cut into $^1/_2$-inch cubes

$^1/_2$ cup heavy cream

2 teaspoons lemon juice

Salt and freshly ground black pepper

Shuck the oysters and reserve them separately from the oyster liquor. Discard the shells.

Melt the butter in a soup pot over medium-low heat. Add the onion, leeks, celery, and fennel and cook until the vegetables begin to soften, 10 to 15 minutes. Add the clam juice, water, and potatoes and simmer until the vegetables are tender, about 15 minutes.

Remove one-quarter of the soup and puree in a blender on high speed until it is very smooth, about 3 minutes. Strain through a fine mesh strainer and return the pureed mixture to the soup base. Stir in the cream and lemon juice and season to taste with salt and pepper.

Just before serving the soup, place over medium heat, stirring occasionally, until very hot. Add the oysters and their liquor and simmer for 1 minute. Ladle the soup into bowls and garnish with the celery leaves and fennel greens.

Serves 6

TO DRINK: Pouilly Fumé or Sancerre

chicken breasts stuffed with goat cheese and olives

Boneless, skinless chicken breasts are a great starting point for a simple weeknight dinner. But when you remove the skin from the chicken, lots of the flavor is lost. Chicken breasts need a little something to give them a jump start, so I stuff them. This assertive mix of fresh goat cheese, briney black olives, and fresh-from-the-garden oregano, flat-leaf parsley, and thyme really do the trick. Stuff the breasts several hours ahead of time and cook them at the last minute.

4 ounces fresh goat cheese

1 tablespoon whole milk

2 garlic cloves, minced

1 tablespoon chopped fresh flat-leaf parsley

1 teaspoon chopped fresh oregano

1 teaspoon chopped fresh thyme

Pinch of red pepper flakes

2 tablespoons chopped imported black olives, such as kalamata or niçoise

Salt and freshly ground black pepper

6 boneless, skinless chicken breast halves (about 6 ounces each)

2 tablespoons extra-virgin olive oil

$1/2$ cup dry white wine, such as Sauvignon Blanc

$1/2$ cup chicken stock

In a small bowl, mash together the goat cheese and milk until smooth. Add the garlic, parsley, oregano, thyme, and red pepper flakes. Mix in the olives and season to taste with salt and pepper.

On the thickest side of each chicken breast, cut a deep, 3-inch-long pocket. Using your fingers, stuff the goat cheese mixture into each pocket. Close by pressing the flesh together and secure with a toothpick, if necessary.

In a large skillet, heat the oil over medium heat. Have ready a lid that is too small for the pan, but will cover all the breasts. Cook the chicken on 1 side until golden brown, 4 to 5 minutes. Turn the breasts, season with salt and pepper, and set the small lid on top of the chicken in the pan. Continue to cook until the chicken is cooked through, 4 to 5 minutes more.

Transfer the chicken to a warm serving platter. Pour the wine into the pan and cook, scraping up the flavorful brown bits stuck to the bottom of the pan. Cook until the wine has reduced by about half, 1 to 2 minutes. Add the chicken stock, season with salt and pepper, and cook until the sauce is reduced to a glossy syrup, about 1 minute.

Drizzle the reduction over the chicken and serve.

Serves 6

TO DRINK: Sauvignon Blanc

grilled chicken breasts with sweet corn and pepper relish

It's the height of summer, you wander into your garden, and it seems that almost overnight sweet bell peppers in jewel-like colors and corn stalks reaching to the sky have overrun the garden. What to do? Make a really colorful, flavorful pepper-and-corn relish to serve with just about every meat, fish, or poultry. The relish is crunchy and acidic and pairs really well with the neutral flavors of grilled chicken breasts. Note that the chicken breasts must marinate for at least two hours before using.

1 lemon

6 boneless, skinless chicken breast halves
(about 6 ounces each)

6 tablespoons extra-virgin olive oil

1 ear fresh corn, kernels removed from
the cob (about 1 cup)

1 red bell pepper, halved, cored, and
cut into $1/4$-inch dice

1 green bell pepper, halved, cored,
and cut into $1/4$-inch dice

1 yellow bell pepper, halved, cored,
and cut into $1/4$-inch dice

1 small red onion, cut into $1/4$-inch dice

2 garlic cloves, minced

3 tablespoons chopped fresh flat-leaf parsley,
plus some whole leaves, for garnish

$1/4$ cup red wine vinegar

Salt and freshly ground black pepper

Peel the lemon with a vegetable peeler. Marinate the chicken breasts in the refrigerator with 2 tablespoons of the olive oil and lemon peel for 2 hours or overnight.

Bring a small saucepan of salted water to a boil over medium-high heat. Add the corn and simmer for 1 minute. Drain and let cool.

To make the relish, combine the corn, bell peppers, onion, garlic, and parsley in a bowl. Mix thoroughly. Add the remaining 4 tablespoons olive oil and vinegar. Season to taste with salt and pepper.

Preheat a charcoal grill.

Grill the chicken breasts until golden on 1 side, 4 to 5 minutes.

Turn the breasts, season with salt and pepper, and continue to grill until golden and cooked through, 4 to 5 minutes more.

To serve, slice each chicken breast on the diagonal into 4 or 5 slices. Top with the relish and garnish with the parsley leaves.

Serves 6

TO DRINK: Rosé or Dolcetto

herb-roasted chicken cooked under a brick

Leave it to the Italians to come up with an ingenious way to cook chicken perfectly: under a brick! Yes, you read that right, it's cooked under a brick. The chicken ends up as flat as a pancake, the meat as moist as can be, and the skin incredibly crisp. Although, traditionally, chicken cooked under a brick isn't brined, I find that brining the chicken overnight makes the final results even more tender.

1 whole chicken (3^1/$_2$ to 4 pounds)

Kosher salt

3 tablespoons chopped fresh flat-leaf parsley

2 tablespoons snipped fresh chives

1 tablespoon chopped fresh lemon verbena (optional)

1^1/$_2$ teaspoons chopped fresh thyme

1^1/$_2$ teaspoons chopped fresh oregano

2 tablespoons extra-virgin olive oil

1 teaspoon grated lemon zest

Freshly ground black pepper

Sprigs of thyme and parsley, for garnish

Wash the chicken and place in a big bowl. For each 1 cup of water, dissolve 1 tablespoon kosher salt. Completely submerge the chicken in the salted water and let it sit in the refrigerator overnight or up to 24 hours. Remove from the refrigerator, drain, and pat dry.

Cut off the wing tips to the second joint and set aside for making stock. Cut down both sides of the backbone to remove the backbone. Reserve the backbone with the wing tips. Remove the excess fat. Flatten the chicken as best you can by pressing on the breast.

Preheat a charcoal grill.

In a small bowl, combine the parsley, chives, lemon verbena, thyme, oregano, olive oil, and lemon zest. Season to taste with salt and pepper. Separate the skin from the breasts and legs of the chicken. Slide the herb mixture between the skin and the meat of the chicken.

Place the chicken, skin side down, on the grill about 4 inches from the coals. Top with a baking sheet. Place a brick on top of the baking sheet and let cook until golden brown, 15 to 20 minutes. Remove the brick and baking sheet and turn the chicken. Continue to cook under the baking sheet and brick until the chicken is done, 15 to 20 minutes more. Remove from the grill and cover with aluminum foil for 10 minutes.

To serve, cut the chicken into pieces, garnish with the herb sprigs, and serve immediately.

Serves 4 to 6

TO DRINK: Pinot Noir, Dolcetto, or Côtes du Rhône

oven-crisped chicken with artichokes and olives

To gussy up a chicken, brine it, cut it down the back and flatten it, then sear the skin side in a really hot ovenproof pan. Pop it into the oven and bake it until it's juicy and moist, with a deliciously crispy skin.

1 lemon

18 small or 6 large artichokes

$1/4$ cup extra-virgin olive oil

Salt and freshly ground black pepper

1 whole chicken ($3^1/2$ to 4 pounds)

1 tablespoon canola, grapeseed, or olive oil

1 cup coarsely ground fresh bread crumbs

2 tablespoons chopped fresh flat-leaf parsley

1 cup dry white wine, such as Sauvignon Blanc

2 cups chicken stock

1 cup cured green olives, such as picholine

Fill a large bowl with cold water. Add the juice of 1 lemon. Remove the tough outer leaves of the artichokes. Cut off the top halves of the artichokes, including all of the prickly leaf points. Remove the tough outer leaves until you get to the very light green leaves. Pare the stem to reveal the light green center. If you are using large artichokes, cut them in half. Halve lengthwise, scoop out the prickly chokes, and discard. Cut in half again. As each artichoke is cut, place in the bowl of lemon water.

In a large, heavy, ovenproof skillet, warm 2 tablespoons of the olive oil over medium heat. Add the artichokes and cook, covered, until they can be easily skewered, 10 minutes. Remove the cover and continue to cook on high heat, tossing frequently, until golden and crispy, 5 minutes. Season with salt and pepper. Set aside.

Cut down both sides of the chicken's backbone and remove. Place the chicken on a work surface with the skin side up. Press on the chicken gently so that it lays flat. Make an incision in each of the chicken thighs, then tuck each leg through the incision. Season on both sides.

Preheat the oven to 500°F. Warm the canola oil in a large, heavy skillet over high heat until the oil is almost smoking. Place the chicken in the pan, skin side down, immediately transfer the pan to the oven, and roast for 10 minutes. Turn the chicken and continue to roast until the juices of the thigh run clear when a skewer is inserted, 25 to 30 minutes. Baste halfway through the roasting.

Meanwhile, place the bread crumbs on a baking sheet and drizzle with the remaining 2 tablespoons olive oil. Season and toss together. Place in the oven and bake, tossing occasionally, until golden and crispy, 8 to 12 minutes. Watch them closely. Remove from the oven and let cool. When cool, add the parsley and toss together.

When the chicken is done, remove from the pan, place on a platter, and cover with foil. Discard any excess fat from the pan.

Place the pan on the stove over medium-high heat. Be careful, as the handle is hot! Add the white wine and reduce by half, 2 to 3 minutes. Add the chicken stock and reduce by one-quarter, or until the sauce coats the back of a spoon. Add the artichokes and olives and heat for 1 to 2 minutes.

To serve, cut the chicken into pieces and place on a platter. Top with the artichokes and olives, and sprinkle with the bread crumbs.

Serves 6

TO DRINK: White Châteauneuf-du-Pape or rosé

chicken ragout with autumn vegetables

In the wine country, autumn brings to mind makeshift vegetable stands set up along country roads. Scrawled hand-lettered signs boast butternut squash, carrots, parsnips, rutabagas, and turnips. This is the right time to get out your favorite braising pan and braise some chicken with all these hearty fall vegetables.

2 tablespoons unsalted butter

4 bacon slices, cut into $^1/_2$-inch dice

1 whole chicken (about 4 pounds),
    cut into 10 pieces

Salt and freshly ground black pepper

4 cups dry white wine, such as Sauvignon Blanc

4 cups chicken stock

3 garlic cloves, minced

2 bay leaves

$^1/_2$ teaspoon chopped fresh thyme

6 sprigs of parsley, tied together

2 parsnips, peeled and cut into 1-inch lengths

2 carrots, peeled and cut into 1-inch lengths

1 medium-size turnip, peeled and
    cut into 8 wedges

1 medium-size rutabaga, peeled and cut
    into 8 wedges

2 tablespoons all-purpose flour

1 tablespoon coarsely chopped fresh
    flat-leaf parsley, for garnish

Melt 1 tablespoon of the butter in a large, heavy casserole over medium heat. Add the bacon and cook until light golden, about 10 minutes. Remove with a slotted spoon to paper towels and set aside. Increase the heat to medium-high. In the same pan, add the chicken in a single layer, with space between the pieces, and season with salt and pepper. Cook until light golden on each side, about 10 minutes. Remove the white meat. Add the bacon and mix well. Increase the heat to high and add the wine, stock, garlic, bay leaves, thyme, and parsley. Bring to a boil, decrease the heat to low, and simmer, covered, for 15 minutes. Place the white meat back in the pan and continue to cook, covered, until the chicken is done, 5 to 10 minutes. Remove the chicken from the pan with tongs and set aside, covered with aluminum foil to keep warm.

Strain the liquid and pour it back into the pan. Discard the solids. Add the parsnips, carrots, turnip, and rutabaga, cover, and cook until the vegetables are tender, about 15 minutes. With a slotted spoon, remove the vegetables from the pan. Increase the heat to high and reduce the broth until 3 cups remain, 5 to 8 minutes. Skim.

In a small bowl, mash together the flour and remaining 1 tablespoon butter with a fork. Bring the liquid to a boil over medium-high heat and, with a whisk, mix the flour and butter into the liquid, simmering, until the liquid thickens and coats a spoon lightly, 2 to 3 minutes.

To serve, heat the sauce over medium-high heat until it is hot. Add the chicken and vegetables and heat through, 3 to 4 minutes. Place the vegetables and chicken on a platter and drizzle the sauce over the top. Garnish with the parsley and serve.

Serves 4 to 6

TO DRINK: White Rhône, Chardonnay, or red Burgundy

penne with tomatoes, spicy fennel sausage, and cream

Okay, let's be honest here—who doesn't love sausage? This pasta, an all-time favorite of mine and many of my students and friends, is made with spicy hot pork and fennel sausage, tomatoes, and a little cream. This dish is a knockout, and you'll find yourself coming back to it again and again.

1 tablespoon extra-virgin olive oil

1 pound sweet Italian pork and
    fennel sausage, crumbled

1 small red onion, chopped

2 garlic cloves, minced

Pinch of red pepper flakes

2 bay leaves

1 teaspoon chopped fresh sage

1 teaspoon chopped fresh rosemary

$^3/_4$ cup dry red wine

$2^1/_2$ cups peeled, seeded, and diced
    tomatoes (fresh or canned) (page 6)

$^3/_4$ cup heavy cream

$^3/_4$ cup grated Parmigiano-Reggiano cheese

Salt and freshly ground black pepper

12 ounces penne or rigatoni pasta

Heat the olive oil in a large skillet over medium heat. Add the sausage and cook until the fat is rendered and the juices have evaporated, 8 to 10 minutes. Add the onion, garlic, red pepper flakes, bay leaves, sage, and rosemary, and cook, stirring occasionally, until the onions are soft, about 15 minutes. Drain off all but 2 tablespoons of fat and discard. Increase the heat to high, add the wine, and boil until it has almost evaporated, 5 minutes. Add the tomatoes and bring to a boil. Decrease the heat to low and simmer until the sauce thickens, 30 to 40 minutes. Remove the bay leaves and discard. Add the cream and half of the Parmigiano and stir together. Season to taste with salt and pepper.

Bring a large pot of salted water to a boil over high heat. Add the penne and cook until al dente, 10 to 12 minutes. Drain the pasta, put it back in the pan, and toss with the tomato sauce. Place on a platter, sprinkle with the remaining Parmigiano, and serve immediately.

Serves 6

TO DRINK: Barbera

pork and artichoke stew

I've never met a stew I didn't love, especially this one, inspired by the Rhône Valley in southern France, where they grow the absolute best artichokes and make deliciously fruity, yet dry, rosé wines—perfect for pairing with this stew. Serve this rib-sticker on a chilly winter night.

1 lemon

6 medium-size artichokes

3 tablespoons extra-virgin olive oil

$^1/_4$ cup water

2 medium-size yellow onions, chopped

3 pounds pork butt, fat removed and
    cut into 2-inch cubes

$1^1/_2$ tablespoons all-purpose flour

Salt and freshly ground black pepper

2 teaspoons chopped fresh oregano,
    plus sprigs for garnish

3 garlic cloves, chopped

1 cup dry white wine, such as Sauvignon Blanc

$1^1/_2$ cups peeled, seeded, and chopped
    tomatoes (fresh or canned) (page 6)

3 cups chicken stock

Fill a large bowl with cold water. Add the juice of 1 lemon. Remove the tough outer leaves of the artichokes. Cut off the top halves of the artichokes, including all of the prickly leaf points. Remove the tough outer leaves until you get to the very light green leaves. Pare the stem to reveal the light green center. Halve lengthwise, then scoop out the prickly chokes and discard. Cut in half again. As each artichoke is cut, place in the bowl of lemon water.

Warm 1 tablespoon of the olive oil in a large skillet over medium heat. Drain the artichokes and add them to the pan, along with the water.

Cover and cook, stirring occasionally, until the artichokes are almost tender, 15 to 20 minutes. Remove and reserve.

Warm 1 tablespoon of the olive oil in a large, heavy casserole over medium heat and cook the onions, stirring occasionally, until light golden, 15 minutes. Remove with a slotted spoon and set aside.

Add the remaining 1 tablespoon olive oil to the casserole and increase the heat to medium-high. Add the pork in a single layer. Do not over-crowd the pan. Cook, turning occasionally, until golden on all sides, 7 to 10 minutes. Sprinkle the pork with the flour and salt and pepper, and continue to cook until the flour is light golden. Return the onions to the pan with the oregano and garlic. Add the wine and cook until reduced by half, 3 minutes. Add the tomatoes and chicken stock and bring to a boil over high heat. Decrease the heat to low and simmer, covered, until the pork is tender, $1^1/_2$ to 2 hours. Add the artichokes and season to taste with salt and pepper. Simmer slowly for 2 minutes. Ladle the stew into soup bowls, garnish with the oregano sprigs, and serve immediately.

Serves 6

TO DRINK: Provençal red or Languedoc red

pork chops with asparagus and morels

If you are a lover of all things delicious, immediately go to the grocery store to buy some pork chops to make this springtime recipe. Brining the chops adds an additional bit of juiciness to the finished dish, while the morels and asparagus add an earthy, nutty flavor. If morels are unavailable, substitute any other wild or cultivated mushrooms.

6 center-cut pork chops (each about 6 ounces and 1 inch thick), trimmed of excess fat

Kosher salt

$1/2$ cup boiling water

$1/4$ ounce dried morel mushrooms or other dried wild mushrooms

$3/4$ pound asparagus, ends trimmed and cut into $1 1/2$-inch lengths

2 tablespoons extra-virgin olive oil

Salt and freshly ground black pepper

$1 1/2$ cups chicken stock

$1/2$ pound fresh morel mushrooms or other fresh wild mushrooms, halved

1 teaspoon chopped fresh thyme, plus sprigs, for garnish

Wash the pork chops and place in a big bowl. For each 1 cup of water, dissolve 1 tablespoon kosher salt. Completely submerge the pork chops in the salted water and let sit in the refrigerator for 1 hour. Remove from the refrigerator, drain, and pat dry.

In a small bowl, combine the $1/2$ cup boiling water and the dried morels. Let cool to room temperature, about 20 minutes. Line a strainer with cheesecloth and drain the mushrooms. Chop the mushrooms and reserve the mushrooms and their liquid separately.

Bring a saucepan of salted water to a boil over medium-high heat. Add the asparagus and cook until tender, yet crisp, 3 to 5 minutes. Drain and reserve.

In a skillet large enough to hold the chops in a single layer without crowding, warm 1 tablespoon of the olive oil over medium heat. Add the pork chops and cook, uncovered, for 5 minutes. Turn them over and season with salt and pepper. Decrease the heat to medium-low and continue to cook, uncovered, turning occasionally, until golden and firm to the touch, 8 to 9 minutes longer. Remove from the pan, place on a warm platter, and cover with aluminum foil.

Pour the chicken stock into a seperate saucepan and boil rapidly over high heat to reduce by half. Set aside.

In the skillet used to cook the pork chops, heat the remaining 1 tablespoon olive oil over medium-high heat. Add the fresh and dried morels and cook until the fresh mushrooms are tender, 3 to 4 minutes. Remove the mushrooms from the pan and reserve with the pork. Increase the heat to high, add the chicken stock, chopped thyme, and mushroom liquid and reduce until it thickens slightly, 3 to 5 minutes. Add the reserved asparagus and warm for 1 minute.

To serve, place the pork chops on individual plates and divide the sauce, asparagus, and mushrooms over the top. Garnish with the thyme sprigs and serve.

Serves 6

TO DRINK: Rioja

pork roasted the tuscan way

This is a monumental tour de force dish that only the Tuscans could create; it is simple but ingenious. Roll up spiced pork in a hollowed-out baguette and roast it. The pork is juicy, the spices are reminiscent of Tuscany, and the bread is crispy and golden. Close your eyes and imagine you are eating in a little trattoria looking out at the hills of Chianti. The best source for buying fennel pollen is at Central Market in Florence. Of course, if that is out of the question, you can buy it online. You can stick with expensive Italian fennel pollen, or take advantage of the new crop of very fragrant fennel pollen being harvested in the California wine country.

2 teaspoons chopped fresh sage

2 teaspoons chopped fresh rosemary

$1/2$ teaspoon freshly ground black pepper

2 garlic cloves, minced

1 teaspoon kosher salt

$1/4$ teaspoon freshly ground black pepper

$1/4$ teaspoon fennel pollen (optional)

$1/4$ cup extra-virgin olive oil

1 pork tenderloin (about $1^1/4$ to $1^1/2$ pounds), trimmed

1 crusty baguette

On a work surface, mince together the sage, rosemary, garlic, salt, black pepper, and fennel pollen. Reserve.

Heat a skillet over medium-high heat. Add 1 tablespoon of the oil. Cook the pork, turning occasionally, until golden on all sides, 8 to 10 minutes. Roll the pork in the herb mixture and set aside. Halve the baguette lengthwise and scoop out the soft insides. Brush the inside of the baguette with the remaining 3 tablespoons olive oil. Place the pork on the inside of the baguette so that the pork is completely enclosed. Trim off the excess ends of the bread. Tie the baguette at 1- to 2-inch intervals with kitchen string.

Preheat the oven to 375°F. Place the pork on a baking sheet and roast until done, 155°F on an instant-read thermometer inserted into the thickest part, 25 to 30 minutes.

Remove from the oven and let rest for 10 minutes. Remove the strings and cut into slices. Serve.

Serves 4

TO DRINK: Fruity Chianti

pork tenderloin with onion, orange, and raisin marmalade

The richness of pork tastes so good with all things sweet. If you have any leftovers (which I doubt), you can always serve it for lunch the next day at room temperature with a fennel and cabbage slaw.

2 large pork tenderloins
    (about 1 pound each)

3 tablespoons extra-virgin olive oil

$1/4$ teaspoon paprika

$1/4$ teaspoon ground cumin

$1/4$ teaspoon ground cloves

Large pinch of cayenne pepper

Salt and freshly ground black pepper

1 navel orange

$1/3$ cup golden raisins

$1/4$ cup sherry vinegar

2 medium-size yellow onions, thinly sliced

2 teaspoons sugar

$1/4$ cup water

$1/2$ cup dry white wine, such as
    Sauvignon Blanc

2 cups chicken stock

3 sprigs of fresh parsley

2 bay leaves

8 whole cloves

Butterfly the pork by slitting it lengthwise just far enough so it opens up to make a flat piece. Flatten slightly. In a bowl, combine 1 tablespoon of the olive oil, paprika, cumin, cloves, and cayenne, and season with black pepper. Rub it over the pork, place in a baking dish, cover, and refrigerate for 2 hours or overnight.

Zest the orange to make 1 teaspoon grated zest. Juice the orange. In a small saucepan, combine the orange zest, orange juice, raisins, and sherry vinegar. Simmer very slowly over low heat, uncovered, for 10 minutes. Heat the remaining 2 tablespoon olive oil in a large skillet over medium heat. Add the onions and cook, stirring occasionally, until very soft, about 20 minutes. Add the raisin mixture, sprinkle with sugar, cover, and continue to sauté very slowly until the onions are very soft, about 30 minutes. Add the water and continue to cook, uncovered, until almost dry, about 20 minutes. Season to taste with salt and pepper. Place the pork on a work surface, cut side up. Season with salt. Spread the onion mixture evenly over the flattened pork. Close up the pork so it is in its original shape and tie at 1-inch intervals with kitchen string.

In a large skillet, bring the white wine, chicken stock, parsley, bay leaves, and whole cloves to a boil over medium-high heat. Add the pork, decrease the heat to low, and simmer until the pork is done, 25 to 30 minutes. Remove the pork and keep warm. Reduce the stock by half and strain. Season with salt and pepper. Remove the strings and slice the meat into $3/4$-inch slices.

Place on a platter and drizzle the sauce on top before serving.

Serves 6

TO DRINK: Granache or Granaccia

grilled leg of lamb with lavender-rosemary rub

Lamb, garlic, lavender, and rosemary all grow together in Provence in the sunny south of France. Make a simple rub of fresh or dry lavender flowers, fresh rosemary, and mint. Slather it all over lamb that you've studded with garlic, and you have the taste of Provence right there on your plate. All you need is a Provençal red wine and a few vegetables and you will have a meal that will please any guest. Note that the lamb must marinate for at least two hours before using.

5- to 6-pound leg of lamb, boned,
    excess fat removed, and butterflied
3 garlic cloves, thinly sliced
2 tablespoons dry or fresh lavender flowers,
    plus sprigs, for garnish
3 tablespoons chopped fresh rosemary
2 tablespoons chopped fresh mint
3 tablespoons extra-virgin olive oil
Salt and freshly ground black pepper

Make 20 small incisions in the lamb in various places. Tuck a slice of garlic into each incision.

In a bowl, combine the lavender flowers, rosemary, mint, and olive oil. Rub the mixture over the lamb and let sit at room temperature for 2 hours, or overnight in the refrigerator.

Preheat a charcoal grill or broiler.

Place the lamb 4 inches from the coals on the grill or under the broiler. Cook until 1 side is golden, about 15 minutes. Season well with salt and pepper. Turn the lamb and continue to cook until medium-rare, 130° to 135°F when tested with an instant-read thermometer, about 15 minutes. Test by cutting into the thickest part. If it is slightly pink inside, remove from the grill. Cover with foil and let rest for 10 minutes.

Slice the lamb into thin slices across the grain and place on a platter. Garnish with the lavender sprigs before serving.

Serves 6 to 8

TO DRINK: Côtes du Rhône, Côte-Rôtie, Saint-Joseph, Cornas, or Crozes-Hermitage

grilled lamb on rosemary skewers with warm fava salad

Rosemary grows like a weed, so here's the perfect thing for a garden that's overgrown with it: pick some long straight rosemary sprigs, strip off the leaves from most of the stem to make skewers, and thread with the lamb. These skewers not only look great, hot from the grill, but the rosemary also flavors the meat.

12 rosemary skewers, 8 to 10 inches long
4 pounds fresh fava beans, in the pods
5 tablespoons extra-virgin olive oil
1 teaspoon grated lemon zest
2 tablespoons lemon juice
1 tablespoon chopped fresh mint,
    plus sprigs, for garnish
Salt and freshly ground black pepper
2½ pounds lamb cubes, cut from
    the leg or loin, trimmed of all fat
6 lemon wedges, for garnish

Soak the rosemary skewers in water for 30 minutes.

Remove the fava beans from their pods and discard the pods. Bring a pot of water to a boil over high heat, add the fava beans, and boil for 30 seconds. Drain, cool, and shell the beans. Reserve.

In a bowl, whisk together 4 tablespoons of the olive oil, the lemon zest, lemon juice, and mint. Season to taste with salt and pepper. Add the fava beans and stir together.

Preheat a charcoal grill.

Thread the lamb onto the rosemary skewers, distributing evenly. Brush the lamb with the remaining 1 tablespoon oil. Grill the lamb, turning occasionally, until the lamb is slightly firm to the touch, 6 to 8 minutes total.

To serve, place the fava beans on a platter. Top with the skewers of lamb. Garnish with the lemon wedges and mint sprigs and serve immediately.

Serves 6

TO DRINK: Châteauneuf-du-Pape

pot-roasted leg of lamb with garlic and olives

Who would have thought of pot-roasting a whole leg of lamb with loads of garlic, tomatoes, olives, and wine? Lulu Peyraud of Domaine Tempier Vineyard in Bandol, a small town near Marseilles, is famous for this dish, and justifiably so. The lamb is so tender that it literally falls apart. Serve with roasted potatoes, tender young green beans, and a big gutsy red Bandol wine.

3 tablespoons extra-virgin olive oil

1 whole bone-in leg of lamb
(5½ to 6 pounds)

Salt and freshly ground black pepper

1 large yellow onion, chopped

1 cup peeled, seeded, and chopped
tomatoes (fresh or canned) (page 6)

24 garlic cloves, crushed

5 sprigs of fresh thyme

1 cup dry white wine, such as
Sauvignon Blanc

1 cup imported black olives,
such as niçoise or kalamata

In a large, heavy pot, warm the olive oil over medium heat. Season the lamb with salt and pepper. Add the lamb to the pan and cook, turning occasionally, until golden brown on all sides, about 30 minutes. Add the onion and, stirring occasionally, cook until golden, about 20 minutes. Decrease the heat to low, add the tomatoes, garlic, thyme, and ¼ cup of the wine, cover, and cook, turning the lamb occasionally, for about 30 minutes. Add another ¼ cup wine and continue to cook for 30 minutes. Add the olives and another ¼ cup wine and continue to cook, turning the lamb occasionally, for 30 minutes more. Repeat 1 more time.

After 2 hours total cooking time, remove the lamb from the pot, cover with aluminum foil, and let rest for 10 minutes. Remove and discard the thyme.

To serve, slice the lamb and place on a platter. Spoon the garlic and sauce over the lamb. Serve immediately, passing the remaining sauce separately.

Serves 6 to 8

TO DRINK: Red Bandol

golden veal with arugula and tomato salad

The combination of peppery arugula, sweet summer tomatoes, lemon, garlic, and extra-virgin olive oil happens to rock my boat. I put this mixture on pizza, chicken paillards, and these crispy, golden veal scaloppine. It's an all-in-one plate, so you don't even need a vegetable on the side.

1 1/4 pounds veal scaloppine,
    cut from the sirloin
1/2 cup all-purpose flour
2 large eggs, beaten lightly together
2 cups dry bread crumbs
Salt and freshly ground black pepper
5 tablespoons extra-virgin olive oil
2 tablespoons lemon juice
1 small garlic clove, minced
2 tablespoons unsalted butter
3 cups very coarsely chopped arugula
2 small tomatoes, cut into 1/2-inch dice
Lemon wedges, for garnish

With a large, flat meat mallet, flatten each piece of veal between two pieces of waxed paper or plastic wrap until the veal is 1/4 inch thick. To bread the veal, place the flour, eggs, and bread crumbs in three separate bowls. Season the flour and bread crumbs with salt and pepper and mix well. Coat both sides of the veal with flour, shaking off the excess. Next, coat the veal with egg, letting the excess drain. Coat both sides of the veal lightly with bread crumbs. Place on baking sheets in the refrigerator until just before cooking.

In a small bowl, whisk together 3 tablespoons of the olive oil, the lemon juice, and garlic to make a vinaigrette. Season to taste with salt and pepper. Reserve.

In a large skillet, heat the remaining 2 tablespoons olive oil and the butter over medium-high heat. Add the veal pieces in a single layer. Do not overcrowd the pan. Sauté the veal pieces, turning occasionally, until they are golden brown on each side, 4 to 6 minutes total.

To serve, place the veal on a platter. Toss the arugula, tomatoes, and vinaigrette together. Top the veal with the salad, garnish with the lemon wedges, and serve immediately.

Serves 6

TO DRINK: Dry rosé

veal chops with olives, capers, and sage

I'm a sucker for veal chops, so I always order them if I see them on a restaurant menu. I also love to make them at home. This simple-to-prepare-at-the-last-moment dish is a great one for entertaining. And if you're on a budget, you can always substitute boned chicken breasts for veal chops with equally delicious results.

Olive oil, for frying

20 large fresh sage leaves

2 tablespoons extra-virgin olive oil

6 rib-eye veal chops (8 to 10 ounces each)

Salt and freshly ground black pepper

3 garlic cloves, minced

1 cup dry white wine

2 cups chicken stock

1 cup imported black or green olives, pitted and very coarsely chopped

1/4 cup capers, drained

2 tablespoons chopped fresh sage

1 tablespoon lemon juice

Warm 1/2 inch olive oil in a skillet over medium-high heat. When the oil is hot, add the sage leaves and cook until crisp, 30 to 60 seconds. Remove from the pan and drain on paper towels. Reserve for garnishing.

Heat 1 tablespoon of the extra-virgin olive oil in a large skillet over medium heat. Add the veal chops and cook until golden, 5 to 6 minutes. Turn the veal chops, season with salt and pepper, and continue to cook until golden and cooked to medium-rare, 5 to 6 minutes. Remove from the pan, place on a warm platter, cover with aluminum foil, and keep warm.

Increase the heat to medium-high, add the remaining 1 tablespoon extra-virgin olive oil and the garlic, and cook until the garlic is soft, about 15 seconds. Add the white wine and simmer until the wine has almost evaporated, 3 to 5 minutes. Add the chicken stock and reduce by half, 3 to 5 minutes. Add the olives, capers, and chopped sage and stir together. Add the lemon juice and salt and pepper to taste.

To serve, place one chop on each plate and spoon the sauce, olives, and capers over the top and around the sides. Garnish with the crisp sage leaves and serve immediately.

Serves 6

TO DRINK: Côtes du Rhône

beef roulade with roasted fennel and sweet peppers

In every wine country I've ever visited, wild fennel grows profusely along the side of the road. This isn't the edible variety, but its flowers certainly perfume the air and remind me of this dish.

6 to 8 slices beef (about 2 pounds),
    cut $1/4$ inch thick from the rump,
    bottom round, or top round

Salt and freshly ground black pepper

1 small carrot

$1/2$ small yellow onion

1 celery stalk

1 small fennel bulb

$1/4$ cup extra-virgin olive oil

1 garlic clove, minced

$3/4$ teaspoon crushed fennel seed

1 tablespoon chopped fennel greens

$1^1/2$ teaspoons grated lemon zest

2 tablespoons chopped fresh flat-leaf parsley

$1/2$ cup fresh bread crumbs

$1^3/8$ cups beef or chicken stock

2 medium-size fennel bulbs, trimmed and
    quartered from top to bottom

2 red bell peppers, cored, seeded,
    and cut into $1^1/2$-inch strips

$1/2$ teaspoon chopped fresh thyme,
    plus sprigs, for garnish

Trim any excess fat from the meat. Place the slices between 2 pieces of waxed paper or plastic wrap and flatten lightly with a meat mallet until $1/8$ inch thick. Season with salt and pepper. Set aside.

Cut the carrot, onion, celery, and small fennel bulb into $1/8$-inch dice. Warm 2 tablespoons of the olive oil in a large skillet over medium heat. Add the diced vegetables and cook until soft, 12 to 15 minutes. Add the garlic and cook for 1 minute. Remove from the pan and place in a bowl with $1/2$ teaspoon of the fennel seed, fennel greens, 1 teaspoon of the lemon zest, the parsley, and bread crumbs. Add 2 tablespoons of the stock and mix just until moistened. Season to taste. Spread the filling on top of the beef, distributing evenly. Roll the beef and tie with kitchen string at 1-inch intervals.

Warm 1 tablespoon olive oil in a skillet over medium-high heat. Brown the meat on all sides, 3 to 5 minutes. Add the remaining $1^1/2$ cups stock, reduce the heat to low, cover, and simmer until the beef is tender when pierced, 45 to 60 minutes.

In the meantime, bring a saucepan of salted water to a boil. Add the quartered fennel and simmer until crisp, yet almost tender, 4 to 5 minutes. Let cool. Preheat the broiler and adjust the rack so that it is 4 to 5 inches from the heat source.

In a bowl, mix the bell peppers, quartered fennel, remaining 1 tablespoon olive oil, and salt and pepper. In a single layer, place the peppers and fennel on a baking sheet and broil for 4 to 5 minutes. Turn and broil until golden and tender, 3 to 5 minutes. Remove from the oven and place in a bowl with the thyme, remaining $1/4$ teaspoon fennel seed, and the remaining $1/2$ teaspoon lemon zest.

Remove the strings from the beef and cut into $1/2$-inch-thick slices. Skim the fat from the pan juices. Reduce the pan juices by one-quarter. Place the beef on a platter and drizzle with the pan juices. Place the peppers and fennel around the edges and garnish with thyme sprigs. Serve.

Serves 6

TO DRINK: Cabernet Franc

beef braised in red wine

Since this recipe calls for a whole bottle of wine, I beg of you—choose something that doesn't break the bank, but also that you would drink—a Cabernet Sauvignon, Merlot, Chianti, Zinfandel, or Côtes du Rhône. The meat is ready when it's fork tender or falls apart when you cut it with a knife. Get ready for some good eating. Note that the meat must marinate for twenty-four hours before using.

2 bay leaves

2 teaspoons black peppercorns, coarsely cracked

5 sprigs of fresh parsley

2$^1/_2$ pounds beef for braising (chuck roast, bottom round roast, or blade roast)

1 yellow onion, quartered

1 carrot, thinly sliced

1 celery stalk, thinly sliced

1 bottle (750 ml) dry red wine

$^1/_4$ cup diced lard or pork fat

2 tablespoons unsalted butter

1 tablespoon extra-virgin olive oil

Salt

$^1/_2$ teaspoon cornstarch

2 to 3 tablespoons water

Tie the bay leaves and peppercorns in a piece of cheesecloth. Tie a piece of string around the parsley. Place the meat in a bowl with the onion, carrot, celery, parsley, bay leaves, peppercorns, and red wine. Let sit in the refrigerator, turning from time to time, for 24 hours.

Preheat the oven to 350°F.

Remove the meat from the marinade and dry well with paper towels. Reserve the marinade. Place the pork fat in a large, heavy ovenproof pan over medium heat and when the fat begins to run, add the butter and olive oil. Add the meat and brown on all sides, 20 minutes. Season with salt.

In the meantime, place the marinade in a saucepan over medium-high heat and reduce by half, 5 to 10 minutes. Add the marinade to the beef, increase the heat to high, and bring to a simmer. Cover and place in the oven. Cook until the meat is really tender and can be cut with a spoon, 2 to 3 hours.

When the meat is done, remove the meat from the pan and place on a warm platter. Cover loosely with aluminum foil to keep warm. Remove and discard the cheesecloth and parsley. Puree the sauce in a food mill or blender. Pour the pureed sauce into a pan and bring to a simmer over medium-high heat. In a small bowl, combine the cornstarch and water. Add to the simmering sauce and stir until it thickens slightly.

To serve, slice the meat and place on a platter. Top with the sauce.

Serves 6 to 8

TO DRINK: Cabernet Sauvignon or Merlot

Sides

spring vegetables with mint and lemon

The bright green colors of fava beans, asparagus, and sugar snap peas signal spring. Add some mint and lemon zest and you have the freshest side dish of the season.

3 pounds fresh fava beans, in the pods
$1/2$ pound asparagus, ends removed and
    cut diagonally into $1^1/_2$- to 2-inch pieces
$1/2$ pound sugar snap peas, ends trimmed
1 tablespoon extra-virgin olive oil
1 teaspoon lemon zest
1 tablespoon chopped fresh mint
Salt and freshly ground black pepper

Remove the fava beans from their pods and discard the pods. Bring a pot of water to a boil over high heat, add the fava beans, and boil for 30 seconds. Remove with a slotted spoon to a bowl, cool, and shell the beans. Place the shelled beans in a bowl and reserve.

Add the asparagus to the pot of boiling water and cook just until tender, 3 to 4 minutes. Remove with a slotted spoon and reserve with the fava beans.

Bring the water to a boil again and add the sugar snap peas. Simmer until almost tender, but still bright green, 1 to 2 minutes. Drain and add the sugar snap peas to the fava beans and asparagus.

In a skillet, warm the olive oil over medium heat. Add the fava beans, asparagus, sugar snap peas, lemon zest, mint, and salt and pepper and stir just until warm, 2 minutes. Serve immediately.

Serves 6 to 8

grilled summer vegetables

Wine country is the perfect place to do lots of summertime grilling because the weather is beautiful both day and night. And with a plethora of fresh vegetables at this time of year, why not grill a bunch to serve with skewers of chicken, lamb, or fish?

6 Japanese eggplant

4 small zucchini

1 yellow bell pepper

1 red bell pepper

$^1/_4$ cup extra-virgin olive oil,
    plus more for brushing
    and drizzling

Salt and freshly ground black pepper

6 slices coarse-textured bread,
    for garnish

2 garlic cloves

Preheat a charcoal grill.

Cut the eggplant and zucchini into $^1/_4$-inch slices lengthwise. Cut the tops and bottoms off the peppers and core. Cut into 1-inch-wide strips.

Place the vegetables in a bowl and drizzle with the olive oil. Season with salt and pepper.

Grill the vegetables until tender, 3 to 4 minutes per side.

Grill the bread until golden on each side. Rub each slice of bread with garlic and brush with olive oil. Sprinkle with salt.

To serve, place the vegetables on a platter. Drizzle with olive oil and garnish with the toasted bread.

Serves 6

grilled asparagus salad with lemon-shallot relish

I grew up eating boiled asparagus. Yes, it was delicious, but then I discovered grilled asparagus. Grilling really brings out the flavor. Top the grilled spears with a relish of lemon juice, shallots, lemon zest, champagne vinegar, and extra-virgin olive oil. The vinaigrette really brings the asparagus alive and the eggs add a dash of color.

2 large eggs
1 teaspoon champagne vinegar
1 tablespoon lemon juice
1 teaspoon freshly grated lemon zest
1 medium-size shallot, minced
7 tablespoons extra-virgin olive oil
Salt and freshly ground black pepper
2¹/₄ pounds large fresh asparagus spears, ends snapped

Fill a small saucepan three-quarters full of water and bring to a boil over high heat. Decrease the heat to medium, add the eggs, and boil for 10 minutes. Remove the eggs and plunge them in a bowl of ice water. Let cool for 10 minutes.

In a small bowl, whisk together the vinegar, lemon juice, lemon zest, shallot, 5 tablespoons of the olive oil, and salt and pepper to make a vinaigrette.

Press the eggs through a coarse sieve into a bowl or chop coarsely with a knife. Reserve.

Prepare a charcoal grill.

With a vegetable peeler, peel the bottom 3 inches of each asparagus spear. Drizzle the asparagus with the remaining 2 tablespoons oil and season with salt. Grill the asparagus, turning occasionally, until golden and tender, yet crisp, 6 to 7 minutes. Place the asparagus on a platter. Drizzle the vinaigrette onto the asparagus, distributing evenly. Sprinkle with the eggs and serve immediately.

Serves 6

braised fennel with orange

This is the stuff that fennel lovers like me dream about—fresh fennel, oranges, and olives. Braise the ingredients together to tenderize the fennel and meld the flavors and serve with roasted chicken or leg of lamb.

6 large fennel bulbs, tops reserved,
    trimmed and quartered
2 tablespoons extra-virgin olive oil
2 teaspoons sugar
1/4 teaspoon crushed fennel seed
1 cup chicken stock
1 tablespoon orange zest
1/2 cup Lucques or picholine olives
Salt and freshly ground black pepper

Chop the feathery tops of the fennel bulbs and reserve 2 tablespoons.

Heat the olive oil in a large skillet over medium-high heat. Add the fennel bulbs, sugar, and fennel seed and cook, stirring occasionally, for 3 minutes. Add the chicken stock, orange zest, olives, and salt and pepper and simmer until the fennel is very tender and the chicken stock has reduced by three-quarters, 8 to 12 minutes. Season with salt and pepper. Add the reserved fennel greens and stir together.

Serves 6

fennel gratin

You can probably tell by now that I love fennel any which way—from raw in salads to braised with orange. Here, I bake it with bread crumbs and Parmigiano-Reggiano. Assemble it ahead and bake at the last minute.

3 pounds fennel bulbs, trimmed and halved
1 teaspoon plus 1 tablespoon unsalted butter
1 tablespoon extra-virgin olive oil
Salt and freshly ground black pepper
1/2 cup dry bread crumbs
1/4 cup grated Parmigiano-Reggiano cheese

Preheat the oven to 400°F.

Bring a pot of salted water to a boil, add the fennel, and simmer until almost soft, 5 to 7 minutes. Let cool. Cut the fennel into 1/2-inch slices. Brush a 2-quart baking dish with 1 teaspoon of the butter. Place the fennel in the baking dish in an even layer. Dot with the remaining 1 tablespoon butter and drizzle with the olive oil. Season with salt and pepper. Top with the bread crumbs and Parmigiano and bake until golden and crispy, 15 to 20 minutes.

Serves 6

gratin of tomatoes, zucchini, and eggplant

Things that grow together usually go together, like eggplant, tomatoes, and zucchini, the flavors reminiscent of the south of France. Serve this gratin alongside grilled, butterflied leg of lamb for the true flavors of Provence. Don't forget a good bottle of Provençal red or rosé wine.

2 medium-size eggplants, cut into $1/3$-inch slices

$1/4$ cup extra-virgin olive oil

12 Roma tomatoes (about $2^1/2$ pounds)

$1/4$ cup chopped fresh parsley

3 garlic cloves

3 medium-size zucchini, cut into $1/3$-inch slices

Salt and freshly ground pepper

$1/2$ cup chicken stock

$1/2$ cup grated Parmigiano-Reggiano cheese

Preheat the oven to 375°F.

Brush the eggplant slices lightly with the olive oil and place on a baking sheet. Bake, turning occasionally, until light golden, 12 to 20 minutes. Reserve.

Bring a large pot of water to a boil over high heat. Boil the tomatoes for 30 seconds. Run under cold water immediately to cool. Peel and slice into $1/3$-inch slices. Reserve.

Chop the parsley and garlic together until the garlic is minced and the parsley is very finely minced. Reserve.

Oil a 13 by 9-inch baking dish and brush with olive oil. Place a row of tomatoes at one of the short ends of the dish. Next, overlap a row of eggplant on top of the tomatoes. Next, place a row of zucchini on top of the tomatoes, overlapping slightly. Sprinkle with some of the garlic and parsley mixture and salt and pepper. Repeat the layering process until the baking dish is filled and all the vegetables are layered. Pour the stock onto the vegetables and sprinkle with the Parmigiano. Bake until the liquid is almost absorbed and the vegetables are tender, 40 to 50 minutes.

Serves 8

long-cooked green beans with tomatoes and garlic

This is what to do with tough, less-than-prime, end-of-season green beans or maybe those green beans that you had big plans for but ended up forgotten in the back of the fridge (we all are guilty of that one). When the summer season is over, but I still want that burst of summer flavor, this is the recipe I always seem to turn to.

2 tablespoons extra-virgin olive oil

$1/4$ cup minced onion

3 garlic cloves, minced

$1^1/2$ pounds green beans, ends trimmed

3 large, ripe tomatoes, peeled, seeded and chopped (page 6)

Salt and freshly ground black pepper

Warm the olive oil in a large skillet over medium heat. Add the onion and cook, stirring occasionally, until soft, 7 to 10 minutes. Add the garlic and continue to stir for 1 minute. Add the green beans and tomatoes, cover, and cook over low heat until the green beans are very soft, 35 to 45 minutes. Season with salt and pepper. Remove the cover and cook until the liquid is almost gone, 3 to 5 minutes.

Serves 6

oven-roasted winter vegetables

In the wine country, the soil is so rich and the climate so temperate that everyone has gardens year-round. Winter root vegetables happen to be my own particular favorite from the garden. Serve them hot from the oven with roasted chicken or as a side dish with your Thanksgiving turkey. You don't need to share this with your guests, but they're packed with essential vitamins and minerals as well as lots of flavor.

$^1/_2$ pound carrots, peeled and
    cut into 1-inch pieces

$^1/_2$ pound Brussels sprouts, trimmed

$^1/_2$ pound rutabagas, peeled and
    cut into 1-inch pieces

$^1/_2$ pound parsnips, peeled and
    cut into 1-inch pieces

$^1/_2$ pound sweet potatoes, peeled
    and cut into 1-inch pieces

1 tablespoon unsalted butter

1 tablespoon extra-virgin olive oil

2 teaspoons chopped fresh thyme

2 teaspoons chopped fresh sage

$^1/_8$ teaspoon freshly grated nutmeg

Salt and freshly ground black pepper

$^1/_2$ cup Marsala wine

Preheat the oven to 450°F.

Bring a pot of salted water to a boil over medium-high heat. Add the carrots and Brussels sprouts and simmer until they give slightly when pierced with a fork, about 5 minutes.

Place the carrots, Brussels sprouts, rutabagas, parsnips, and sweet potatoes in a large roasting pan. Melt the butter in a small saucepan and stir in the oil, thyme, sage, and nutmeg. Drizzle the butter mixture over the vegetables and toss to coat them completely. Season to taste with salt and pepper. Pour the Marsala into the bottom of the roasting pan. Cover tightly with aluminum foil and bake in the oven for 40 minutes.

Remove the foil, toss the vegetables, and continue to cook until the Marsala is evaporated and the vegetables can be easily pierced with a knife, 20 to 30 minutes.

Place the roasted vegetables on a platter and serve immediately.

Serves 6

artichokes stewed with olive oil, lemon, and plenty of garlic

In the early spring, thorny blossoms called artichokes shoot from silver-green leaves that resemble saw blades. If it's a good year, artichokes are harvested again in the fall. When there's a surplus, here's one solution: Braise them in olive oil, lemon, and lots of garlic. Then store them in the refrigerator and use for salads, on pizza, on an antipasto platter, on a crostini, or just eat them straight from the jar with a big spoon.

5 lemons

36 small artichokes or 12 medium-size artichokes

10 sprigs of fresh thyme

5 bay leaves

20 garlic cloves, halved

$^3/_4$ cup extra-virgin olive oil

1 teaspoon salt

With a vegetable peeler, remove the zest from the lemons.

Prepare a large bowl of water to which you have added the juice of 1 lemon. Remove the tough outer leaves of the artichokes. Working with 1 artichoke at a time, cut off the top halves of the artichokes, including all of the prickly leaf points. Remove the tough outer leaves of the artichoke until you get to the very light green leaves. Pare the stem to reveal the light green center. Cut each one in half lengthwise, then scoop out the prickly chokes and discard. If you are using large artichokes, cut in half again. As each is cut, place in the bowl of lemon water.

Drain the artichokes and place them in a saucepan with the juice of the remaining 4 lemons, the lemon peel, thyme, bay leaves, garlic, olive oil, and salt. Add water just to cover. Cover the pan with a piece of parchment paper and weight the parchment with a small plate that fits inside the pan. Over medium-high heat, bring to a boil, decrease the heat to medium, and simmer for 5 minutes. Turn off the heat and let the pan cool completely, about 1 hour.

Divide the mixture between 2 quart jars and store in the refrigerator until ready to use. They will keep for 2 weeks in the refrigerator.

Makes 2 quarts

shallots agrodolce

Agrodolce means "sour and sweet" in Italian, and that's just what these shallots are. The shallots are sweet from the raisins, cloves, and sugar and sour from the red wine vinegar and lemon. Serve these with roast pork or pan-fried duck breasts.

2 pounds shallots
1 cup dry red wine
$^1/_2$ cup red wine vinegar
1 cup water
$^1/_4$ cup dark raisins
2 bay leaves
6 whole cloves
1 tablespoon grated lemon zest
1 tablespoon sugar
Salt and freshly ground black pepper

Bring a pot of water to a boil over high heat. Add the shallots and cook for 1 minute. Drain and peel. Trim off the root end very close to the root.

Place the shallots in a skillet and add the red wine, vinegar, water, raisins, bay leaves, cloves, lemon zest, and sugar. Bring to a boil over high heat. Decrease the heat to low and simmer, uncovered, until tender, 20 minutes. Cool. Remove and discard the cloves and bay leaves.

To serve, spoon the shallots, raisins, and as much of the sauce as desired into a bowl.

Serves 6

grain pilaf with nuts and dried fruit

This is a nice change from potatoes or simple steamed rice: millet, bulgur, and basmati rice studded with toasted pistachios and dried apricots, apples, and cherries. It's earthy, crunchy, really nutritious, and the ideal accompaniment to roast chicken, roast pork, or oven-roasted duck breasts. Plus, the colors are beautiful.

1 tablespoon canola or vegetable oil

$1/2$ cup bulgur

$3/4$ cup basmati rice

$1/4$ cup millet

$1/4$ cup dried apricots, chopped

$1/4$ cup dried apples, chopped

$1/4$ cup dried cherries, chopped

Salt and freshly ground black pepper

2 cups chicken stock

1 cup water

$3/4$ cup shelled pistachios, toasted
(page 7)

Preheat the oven to 375°F.

Heat the oil in a saucepan over medium heat. Add the bulgur, rice, and millet and stir until the grains are coated and hot, 1 to 2 minutes. Increase the heat to high. Add the apricots, apples, cherries, $3/4$ teaspoon salt, pepper, stock, and water and bring to a boil. Decrease the heat to low and simmer, covered, until the grains are tender and the liquid is absorbed, 25 minutes. Add the pistachios and fluff with a fork to mix. Season to taste with salt and pepper. Serve immediately.

Serves 6

fire-roasted potatoes with cumin and garlic

I know I'm not alone in saying that I never met a potato I didn't like. Roasted garlic, cumin, coriander, sweet paprika, red pepper flakes, and pimenton make potatoes you can't stop eating. Pimenton is smoked paprika and adds a nice smokiness to the dish.

3 pounds small new red potatoes

6 whole garlic cloves, in their skins

Salt and freshly ground black pepper

2 tablespoons cumin seed

2 teaspoons coriander seed

$^1/_2$ teaspoon sweet paprika

Large pinch of pimenton

$^1/_4$ teaspoon red pepper flakes

$^1/_4$ cup extra-virgin olive oil

Preheat the oven to 375°F.

Wash the potatoes, but do not dry them. Place in a roasting pan with the garlic, season with salt and pepper, and toss together. Cover with aluminum foil and bake until the potatoes and garlic are tender, 1 hour. When the garlic is tender and cool, remove the cloves from the skins. Discard the skins and chop the garlic. Reserve.

In the meantime, place the cumin seed and coriander seed in a small dry skillet over medium heat. Toast until light golden, 1 to 2 minutes. Place in a spice or coffee grinder with the paprika, pimenton, red pepper flakes, $^1/_2$ teaspoon salt, and pepper and process until coarsely ground.

Prepare a charcoal grill.

Cut the potatoes in half. Brush or dip the cut side of the potato in olive oil, using 2 tablespoons oil total. Grill the potatoes until golden, 3 to 5 minutes. Place in a bowl and toss with the remaining 2 tablespoons olive oil, the cumin-coriander spice mixture, and the roasted garlic.

Serves 6

Desserts

summer melons in sweet spiced wine

A late-harvest wine means that the grapes have been allowed to stay on the vine after the regular harvest, developing a beneficial, if scary-sounding mold called botrytis. As the fruit withers on the vine, the juice concentrates with greater sweetness, a perfect match for dessert. In this recipe, I have made a syrup with a late-harvest wine to use as a sauce for the sweet summer melons. Chilled and served on a warm summer evening under the stars, this simple dessert is so refreshing.

1 orange

1 1/2 cups late-harvest dessert wine,
    such as Riesling, Gewürztraminer,
    Muscat, or Sauternes

1 tablespoon honey

1/2 vanilla bean, split and scraped

4 slices fresh ginger, cut 1/4 inch long

5 pounds assorted melons, such as
    cantaloupe, honeydew, Crenshaw,
    casaba, and Persian

Peel the orange with a vegetable peeler, making sure there is no white pith on the back of the peel. Juice the orange. Bring the orange juice, orange peel, wine, honey, vanilla bean, and ginger to a boil in a saucepan over high heat. Decrease the heat to low and simmer for 5 minutes. Remove from the heat and remove the orange peel, vanilla bean, and ginger, and discard. Let cool for 30 minutes.

In the meantime, using a melon baller, form balls of melon and place in a large glass bowl. Pour the orange-infused wine over the melon and let sit in the refrigerator for 1 hour, until the melon is chilled.

To serve, ladle the melon into bowls and pour the sauce over the melon.

Serves 6

TO DRINK: Serve the same wine you used in the recipe

pears and figs with pecorino, walnuts, and honey

If you don't have time to make dessert, but you still want a bite of something sweet, try this. It's really more of a composed plate, rather than a true recipe: wedges of fresh pecorino cheese drizzled with sweet chestnut honey and topped with toasted walnuts, pears, and fresh figs. You'll find a variety of figs in the market: Missions are a dark purple fig with a rose-colored center; plump Calimyrna figs have white flesh and green skin; Kadotas are small figs, with white flesh and thick green skin. You can use all one type or an assortment for this dessert.

6-ounce piece pecorino cheese

1 ripe red Bartlett pear

2 ripe green Bartlett pears

12 ripe assorted figs

6 fig leaves, for garnish

3 tablespoons chestnut honey
   or other flavorful honey

$1/2$ cup fresh new crop walnut halves,
   toasted (page 7)

Preheat the oven to 350°F.

Shave pieces of the pecorino, using three-quarters of the cheese. Halve the pears and core them. Cut each half into 3 wedges. Halve the figs.

To serve, place the fig leaves on a large platter. Top with the pears. Disperse the figs, some with the cut side up and some with the cut side down, between the pears. Top with the shaved pecorino. Warm the honey in a saucepan over low heat, 1 minute. Drizzle the honey over the top. Scatter the walnut halves on top before serving.

Serves 6

TO DRINK: Vin Santo

peach and blueberry crisp

Crisps tend to be my no-brainer dessert. Whenever I make crisp topping, I make some extra to freeze. Then, when I need a quick dessert, all I have to do is to cut up the fruit, toss it with some sugar, and sprinkle with the crisp topping. Peeling the peaches is the only "work" with this recipe. I've recently found a nifty little vegetable peeler with serrated blades that does a great job on peaches. But if I'm lazy or strapped for time, I substitute nectarines, which don't have to be peeled.

CRISP TOPPING

$^3/_4$ cup pecans or walnuts, toasted
　　(page 7)
1$^1/_2$ cups all-purpose flour
$^1/_2$ cup firmly packed brown sugar
$^1/_4$ teaspoon freshly grated nutmeg
$^1/_2$ cup (1 stick) unsalted butter, at room
　　temperature

FRUIT FILLING

3 pounds peaches
2 cups blueberries
3 tablespoons all-purpose flour
2 tablespoons granulated sugar

To make the topping, place the nuts in a food processor and pulse a few times until the nuts are in $^1/_4$-inch pieces. Remove the nuts and reserve. In a bowl, mix together the flour, brown sugar, and nutmeg. Add the dry ingredients and butter to the food processor and pulse until it just begins to hold together. Add the nuts and pulse 3 or 4 more times until mixed.

Preheat the oven to 375°F.

To make the filling, peel the peaches, using a knife or blanching the peaches to loosen the skin. To blanch them: Bring a large saucepan of water to a boil over high heat. Boil the peaches for 20 seconds. Remove from the water. When cool enough to handle, peel the peaches and cut them into $^3/_4$-inch wedges. Discard the pits.

In a bowl, toss together the peaches, blueberries, flour, and sugar until well mixed. Place the fruit in a 2- to 2$^1/_2$-quart baking dish and sprinkle evenly with the crisp topping. Bake in the center of the oven until a skewer inserted into the center goes in without any resistance, the top is golden, and the fruit mixture is bubbling around the edges, 35 to 40 minutes. Remove from the oven and let cool for 20 minutes before serving.

To serve, spoon the crisp into individual dessert dishes.

Serves 8

TO DRINK: Demi-sec Champagne or sparkling wine

fresh cherries with cassis zabaglione

I always say that if cherries didn't have pits, they'd be dangerous. When I eat cherries, having to remove their pits is all that slows me down enough to give others a fighting chance to get some of the fruit for themselves. So when May comes around and it's cherry season, I'm in heaven. I eat them fresh, stir them into ice creams, and bake them into any number of cakes and pies. I just love them matched up with zabaglione, one of Italy's great desserts. This ethereal foamy custard sauce is traditionally made with egg yolks, sugar, and Marsala wine. In this recipe I've substituted crème de cassis for the Marsala. The black currant-flavored liqueur is a nice match for the cherries.

4 large egg yolks

$1/4$ cup sugar

2 tablespoons water

6 tablespoons crème de cassis

2 pounds cherries, pitted

Have a saucepan of barely simmering water ready 15 minutes before serving. To make the zabaglione, whisk the egg yolks, sugar, and water together in a large bowl. Whisk in the crème de cassis and set the bowl over the pan of barely simmering water. Don't let the water touch the bottom of the bowl. Whisk constantly until the mixture is thick, frothy, and begins to hold soft peaks, and there is no liquid left at the bottom of the bowl, 5 to 8 minutes.

To serve, divide the cherries among 6 large wine glasses. Spoon the zabaglione onto the cherries and serve immediately.

Serves 6

TO DRINK: Sparkling wine, Auslese, or Spätlese

creamy summer berry and lemon gratin

Every time I teach this dessert in class, my students almost lick their plates. It's creamy, not too sweet, lemony, studded with summer berries, and comforting—everything a dessert should be. It can also be made with peaches or nectarines, and in the winter, blood or navel oranges.

4 lemons

1 1/2 cups whole milk

5 large egg yolks

1 teaspoon cornstarch

1/3 cup granulated sugar

2 tablespoons all-purpose flour

1/2 teaspoon vanilla extract

1 tablespoon lemon juice

1 tablespoon unsalted butter,
    at room temperature

1/2 cup mascarpone cheese

4 cups mixed berries, such as blueberries,
    blackberries, raspberries, and
    boysenberries

2 tablespoons confectioners' sugar

Peel the lemons with a vegetable peeler, avoiding the white pith. Scald the milk in a saucepan over medium heat. Add the lemon peel and remove from the heat. Let sit for 1 hour. After 1 hour, strain the milk to remove the lemon peel and discard the peel.

In a bowl, beat the egg yolks until light and fluffy. In another bowl, combine the cornstarch, sugar, and flour. Add this mixture to the egg yolks and beat until light and fluffy, about 1 minute.

Scald the milk a second time and then add it slowly to the eggs, whisking constantly. Place the mixture back in the saucepan and, over low heat, stirring constantly, cook until the mixture thickens and bubbles form around the edges. Remove from the heat and whisk in the vanilla, lemon juice, and butter. Fold in the mascarpone until well incorporated.

Preheat the broiler.

Divide the custard mixture among 6 or 8 individual gratin or tartlet dishes, 5 inches in diameter. Press the berries into the custard mixture. Sift the confectioners' sugar over the tops. Broil until the tops are golden brown, 1 to 2 minutes. Serve hot or at room temperature.

Serves 6 to 8

TO DRINK: Late-harvest Riesling or late-harvest Gewürztraminer

baked apples filled with dried fruits and nuts

Autumn in wine country—when the summer heat finally gives way to cool, clear days and chilly nights—is the time for harvesting grapes and picking pears, walnuts, and apples. These warm-from-the-oven sweet baked apples, stuffed with dried fruit and nuts, are finished with a dollop of mascarpone that oozes down the sides when baked. Irresistible!

6 apples, such as Delicious, Cortland, Rome Beauty, or McIntosh

$1/2$ cup firmly packed brown sugar

5 tablespoons unsalted butter, melted

$3/4$ cup water

$3/4$ teaspoon ground cinnamon

$3/4$ teaspoon grated lemon zest

$1/4$ cup walnuts, toasted and coarsely chopped (page 7)

$1/4$ cup dried apples, chopped

$1/4$ cup golden raisins

$1/4$ cup dried apricots, chopped

4 amaretto cookies, crushed

$3/4$ cup mascarpone cheese

Preheat the oven to 375°F.

Core the apples, cutting to within $1/2$ inch of the bottom (leave the bottom intact). Cut a $1/2$-inch-thick slice off the stem end of each and set aside.

In a small pan over medium-high heat, combine 6 tablespoons of the brown sugar, 3 tablespoons of the butter, the water, $1/2$ teaspoon of the cinnamon, and the lemon zest. Bring to a boil, stirring to dissolve the sugar, to make a syrup. Remove the syrup from the heat and set aside.

In a bowl, mix together the walnuts, dried apples, raisins, apricots, the remaining 2 tablespoons brown sugar, the remaining $1/4$ teaspoon cinnamon, the remaining 2 tablespoons melted butter, and three-quarters of the crushed amaretto cookies. Reserve the remaining crushed cookies. Fill the apples with the mixture, distributing evenly. Place the tops of the apples on the filling.

Place the apples in a 2-quart baking dish and pour the syrup over them. Cover with aluminum foil and bake until the apples are tender, about 30 minutes. Baste with the pan juices and continue to cook, the apples covered with aluminum foil, until the apples are just tender, 10 to 15 minutes, depending upon the variety of the apple.

When the apples are done, remove the foil and spoon some of the syrup over the top.

To serve, spoon the mascarpone into the hole on the top of each hot baked apple, distributing evenly. Sprinkle the mascarpone with the reserved crushed amaretto cookies. Drizzle the syrup from the pan around the edges before serving.

Serves 6

TO DRINK: Tokaji Aszú

lemon cloud tart

After a meal, something made with lemon is one of the most refreshing desserts. This tart is based on classic lemon meringue pie, but better. Imagine a buttery, flaky crust, an intensely tart and sweet lemon filling, and an airy, vanilla meringue. Plus, if you eat it standing up, there are no calories!

SHORT CRUST PASTRY

1¼ cups all-purpose flour

1 tablespoon sugar

Pinch of salt

1 teaspoon grated lemon zest

½ cup (1 stick) plus 2 tablespoons
    unsalted butter, at room temperature
    for 15 minutes, cut into small pieces

1 tablespoon ice water

FILLING

4 large egg yolks

⅓ cup sugar

⅓ cup lemon juice

3 tablespoons grated lemon zest

3 tablespoons unsalted butter, melted

⅓ cup blanched almonds, toasted
    and ground (page 7)

MERINGUE

3 large egg whites, at room temperature

¾ cup sugar

½ teaspoon vanilla extract

To make the pastry, in a food processor, mix the flour, sugar, and salt with a few pulses. Add the lemon zest and butter and pulse until the mixture resembles cornmeal. Add as much ice water as needed until the pastry just holds together in a ball, up to 1 tablespoon. Remove from the processor, flatten into a 6-inch disk, and wrap in plastic wrap. Refrigerate for 30 minutes.

Press the pastry evenly into the bottom and sides of a 9-inch tart pan. Set the tart shell in the freezer for 30 minutes.

Preheat the oven to 400°F.

Line the pastry with parchment paper and scatter 1 cup of dry beans or pie weights over the parchment. Bake the tart shell until the top edges are light golden, 10 to 15 minutes. Remove the parchment and weights, decrease the heat to 375°F, and continue to bake until the shell is light golden, 15 to 20 minutes more.

While the tart shell is baking, make the filling. Beat the egg yolks and sugar until they form a stiff ribbon. Stir in the lemon juice and grated zest, then the melted butter and almonds. Pour the filling into the prebaked shell and bake until a skewer inserted into the center comes out clean, 20 to 30 minutes. Remove the tart from the oven and let cool completely.

Increase the oven temperature to 450°F.

To finish the tart, make the meringue. Place the egg whites in a clean bowl and beat until soft peaks form. Add the sugar, a little at a time, and continue beating until they form stiff peaks. Fold in the vanilla. Spread the meringue on top of the filling, making peaks. Bake the tart in the middle of the oven until the meringue is golden brown, about 7 minutes. Chill the tart until set, about 1 hour.

Makes one 9-inch tart, to serve 8

TO DRINK: Sauternes

warm nectarine and polenta tart with soft cream

I have the fondest memories of my grandfather's orchard. He'd pick the fruit and my grandmother would use it to simmer big batches of jams and jellies and bake all kinds of pies. I don't think my grandmother put polenta into her pastry, but I guarantee if she had she would have loved the crunchy results. This tart, filled with warm, sweet nectarines, is inspired by ones I've eaten in northern Italy. Make sure the nectarines aren't too ripe and juicy or the bottom of the crust will be soggy. Talk about heavenly!

FILLING

2 pounds medium-ripe nectarines, pitted and cut into $1/4$-inch slices

2 tablespoons all-purpose flour

$1/3$ cup granulated sugar

$1/4$ teaspoon freshly grated nutmeg

DOUGH

$1/2$ cup (1 stick) plus 3 tablespoons unsalted butter, at room temperature

$3/4$ cup granulated sugar

3 large egg yolks

$13/4$ cups all-purpose flour

$1/2$ cup polenta

Pinch of salt

TOPPING

1 cup heavy cream

2 tablespoons confectioners' sugar

$1/4$ teaspoon vanilla extract

To make the filling, toss the nectarines with the flour, granulated sugar, and nutmeg in a bowl. Reserve.

To make the dough, cream the butter and granulated sugar in a food processor until well blended, about 1 minute. Add the egg yolks, 1 at a time, pulsing after each addition. Sift together the flour, polenta, and salt and mix into the creamed mixture. Mix until the dough comes together. Halve the dough. Wrap 1 half in plastic wrap and refrigerate. Press the remaining dough half evenly into the bottom and sides of an $81/2$-inch tart pan. Evenly spoon the nectarines into the tart shell.

Preheat the oven to 375°F.

Remove the other dough half from the refrigerator. On a floured surface, roll out the chilled dough $1/4$ inch thick. With a shaped cookie cutter, such as a heart, cut as many shapes as you possibly can from the rolled dough. Arrange them on the nectarines, with the points of the hearts facing the tart's center, in concentric circles, overlapping slightly. Bake until golden, 35 to 40 minutes. Cool on a rack.

To make the topping, whip the heavy cream until soft peaks are formed. Sift the confectioners' sugar on top of the cream, add the vanilla, and fold together. Serve the tart warm, topped with the cream.

Serves 8

TO DRINK: Late-harvest Viognier

rustic red-and-green plum tart

If you're afraid of making puff pastry, this dessert's for you. This tart uses the simplest, most foolproof, no-brainer puff pastry recipe known to man, and the results are fantastic. The dough can be stored in the refrigerator for up to three days and frozen for a couple of weeks. Imagine the glory of announcing in your most blasé voice, "Oh, you like the puff pastry? I made it myself. No big deal." I use this dough with all kinds of fresh fruits. For plums, I suggest Greengage for the green variety and Santa Rosa for the red.

PASTRY

1 cup all-purpose flour

1/3 cup cake flour

1/4 teaspoon salt

3/4 cup (1 1/2 sticks) unsalted butter,
     cut into 1/2-inch pieces

2 teaspoons lemon juice

1/3 cup ice water

TOPPING

5 or 6 medium-ripe yellow or green plums,
     halved, pitted, and thinly sliced

5 or 6 medium-ripe purple or red plums,
     halved, pitted, and thinly sliced

1/4 cup granulated sugar

2 tablespoons unsalted butter, melted

1/4 cup apricot jam, melted and strained

1 cup heavy cream

2 tablespoons confectioners' sugar

1/4 teaspoon vanilla extract

To make the pastry, 1 hour before using, mix the all-purpose flour, cake flour, and salt, and place in the freezer. Place the butter in a bowl and also place it in the freezer 1 hour before using.

Transfer the cold flour mixture to a food processor. Add the frozen butter and pulse several times until half of the butter is the size of peas and the remaining is smaller. Turn the contents onto a work surface, marble if possible. Make a well in the center. Combine the lemon juice and ice water and add to the cold flour and butter. Gather as best you can to make a ball. Press the dough together as best

you can to form a rough 4 by 6-inch rectangle. There will be large chunks of butter showing.

Roll out the dough into a 5 by 7-inch rectangle, 1/2 inch thick. Fold the narrow ends to meet in the center. Fold in half again so that there are 4 layers. Turn the dough a quarter of a turn and roll again to form a 1/2-inch-thick rectangle. This is your first turn. Repeat the rolling and folding process 2 more times. For the fourth turn, roll the dough and fold it into thirds as you would a business letter. Wrap in plastic wrap and refrigerate for 45 to 60 minutes.

Preheat the oven to 400°F.

To make the topping, combine the plums and 3 tablespoons of the sugar in a bowl. Roll the pastry into a 12-inch circle and place on a baking sheet. Trim and crimp the edges. Sprinkle the dough with the remaining 1 tablespoon sugar. Place the plums in an overlapping decorative pattern in a single layer. Brush with the melted butter and bake in the center of the oven. After 10 minutes, decrease the heat to 375°F and continue to bake until golden and crisp, 25 to 35 minutes. Remove from the oven and brush with the jam. Let cool for 10 minutes.

To serve, whip the heavy cream until soft peaks are formed. Sift the confectioners' sugar on top of the cream, add the vanilla, and fold together. Serve with the tart.

Makes one 10-inch tart, to serve 6 to 8

TO DRINK: Late-harvest Riesling

warm chocolate-walnut tart

I am not a card-carrying chocoholic, but all my friends and family are, so I sure know how to make chocolate desserts. I like this one so much because it's insanely chocolaty, but not so sweet that you can only eat a couple of bites. Even after a big meal, this warm tart will be gobbled up. I add lots of toasted walnuts, and bake it in a crust that seems to dissolve as soon as it reaches your mouth. An old tawny port would complement it nicely. But die-hard chocolate lovers would probably enjoy a big glass of ice-cold milk just as much.

$1/4$ cup ($1/2$ stick) unsalted butter,
    cut into 8 pieces

5 ounces bittersweet chocolate,
    chopped

1 cup dark corn syrup

$1/4$ cup granulated sugar

3 large eggs

2 tablespoons brandy or Cognac

2 cups walnut halves, toasted (page 7)

1 prebaked 9-inch Short Crust Pastry
    (page 191)

1 cup heavy cream, for topping

2 tablespoons confectioners' sugar,
    for topping

$1/4$ teaspoon vanilla extract,
    for topping

Preheat the oven to 350°F.

In a bowl set over a pan of simmering water, melt the butter and chocolate, stirring until smooth. Remove from the pan and transfer to a large bowl. In another saucepan over medium-high heat, stir together the corn syrup and granulated sugar until boiling. Add to the chocolate. In a bowl, whisk together the eggs and brandy until foamy; add to the chocolate mixture along with the walnuts. Stir well. Pour into the prebaked tart shell and bake until a skewer inserted into the center comes out clean, 35 to 40 minutes.

Remove the tart from the oven and let cool until warm, 15 to 20 minutes. In the meantime, whip the cream to soft peaks and flavor with 1 tablespoon of the confectioners' sugar, and the vanilla.

Cut the tart into wedges, dust the top with the remaining 1 tablespoon confectioners' sugar, and serve with the soft cream.

Makes one 9-inch tart, to serve 8 to 10

TO DRINK: Old tawny port

olive oil and orange-essence cake with soft cream

This is the lightest, most delicate cake you can imagine, made with olive oil, Muscat, orange zest, and orange flower water (available at Middle Eastern groceries or online). Olive oil is used in place of butter, so it's a "healthier," lighter, more delicate cake. The wine gives it a subtle, floral sweetness with hints of orange blossom and honeysuckle that pairs beautifully with the orange flower water. It's a single-layer cake that doesn't need frosting. You'll find it's a perfect cake to enjoy with coffee or tea.

5 large eggs, separated

$^3/_4$ cup granulated sugar

2 tablespoons grated orange zest

$^1/_3$ cup extra-virgin olive oil

$^1/_3$ cup sweet Muscat, late-harvest Riesling, or Gewürztraminer wine

$2^1/_2$ tablespoons orange flower water

1 cup sifted all-purpose flour

$^1/_4$ teaspoon salt

$^1/_2$ teaspoon cream of tartar

1 cup heavy cream, for topping

2 tablespoons confectioners' sugar, for topping

$^1/_4$ teaspoon vanilla extract, for topping

Butter and flour a 9-inch springform pan. Preheat the oven to 350°F.

Beat the egg yolks with half the granulated sugar until well ribboned, about 2 minutes. Beat in the orange zest, slowly whisk in the olive oil in drops, and finally, add the wine and flower water. Mix together the flour and salt and beat into the egg mixture.

Beat the egg whites with the cream of tartar until they hold soft peaks. Beat in the remaining granulated sugar until the whites hold stiff peaks. Stir 1 cup of the beaten whites into the batter and then gently fold in the rest of the whites. Pour into the prepared pan and bake for 20 minutes. Decrease the heat to 300°F and continue to bake another 20 minutes. Turn off the oven, cover the top of the cake with a round of buttered parchment paper, and leave in the oven for another 10 minutes. Remove from the oven and let cool in the pan on a rack.

To serve, whip the cream to soft peaks and add 1 tablespoon of the confectioners' sugar and the vanilla. Slice the cake and serve a wedge of the cake with a dollop of the cream on the side, dusted with some of the remaining 1 tablespoon confectioners' sugar.

Serves 8 to 10

TO DRINK: Muscat

little lemon cakes with soft cream

These little lemon miracles (I mean cakes) create two layers of completely different textures when they bake. On the bottom: a spongy, soufflé-like cake layer. On the top: tart lemon curd. A dollop of softly whipped cream adds just the right sweetness and richness, while the raspberries add a gorgeous punch of color. I promise you will love these fun little cakes. A big hug to my best chef friend, Gary Danko, for inspiring this recipe.

Melted butter, as needed, for brushing

Granulated sugar, as needed, for dusting

5 tablespoons unsalted butter

6 tablespoons plus $^3/_4$ cup granulated sugar

5 large eggs, separated

Grated zest of 2 lemons

6 tablespoons all-purpose flour

$1^1/_4$ cups whole milk

$^2/_3$ cup lemon juice, at room temperature

1 cup heavy cream, for topping

2 tablespoons confectioners' sugar, for dusting

$^1/_4$ teaspoon vanilla extract, for topping

Raspberries, for garnish (optional)

Brush 8 ramekins, 5 ounces each, with butter. Dust the inside of each of the ramekins with granulated sugar and tap out the excess. Set aside.

Preheat the oven to 325°F.

Cream the butter and the 6 tablespoons granulated sugar until light in color and texture, 1 to 2 minutes. Add the egg yolks, 1 at a time, beating well after each addition. Stir in the lemon zest and flour. Add the milk and lemon juice and mix thoroughly. In a separate bowl, whip the egg whites to soft peaks form. Add the remaining $^3/_4$ cup sugar. Continue to whip until stiff peaks form. Fold into the lemon mixture. Evenly divide the mixture among the prepared ramekins. Place the ramekins in a large baking pan and pour in boiling water to reach 1 inch up the sides. Bake until set, light brown, and a skewer inserted into the center comes out clean, 30 minutes. Cool completely.

Whip the cream to soft peaks and add 1 tablespoon of the confectioners' sugar and the vanilla.

To serve, unmold the individual cakes onto dessert plates. Top with the cream and dust with the remaining confectioners' sugar. Garnish with raspberries and serve immediately.

Serves 8

TO DRINK: Late-harvest Riesling

warm little chocolate cakes with soft centers

This dessert should be illegal! Here's the idea if you can handle it: as you tuck into your own fudgy chocolate cake, the warm, unctuous, molten center oozes out and acts as a counterpoint to the delicate vanilla custard sauce. The best part is that the unbaked cakes can hold in the fridge all day (tightly covered in plastic wrap) until you are ready to bake them. Master this vanilla custard sauce, the French pastry classic known as crème anglaise, as it puts scores of beautiful desserts over the top.

CUSTARD SAUCE

1¹/₂ cups whole milk

3 tablespoons granulated sugar

¹/₂ vanilla bean, split and scraped

3 large egg yolks

CAKES

9 ounces bittersweet chocolate, finely chopped

6 tablespoons unsalted butter

2 tablespoons Cognac or brandy

¹/₃ cup granulated sugar

4 large eggs, separated

3 tablespoons cake flour

Confectioners' sugar, for dusting

Fresh raspberries or currants, for garnish

To make the custard, in a saucepan over medium heat, warm the milk, sugar, and vanilla bean, stirring constantly to dissolve the sugar. In a small bowl, whisk the egg yolks to break them up, but don't make them foam. Whisk a little of the hot milk into the egg yolks to warm them. Return the eggs to the pan and cook the custard, stirring constantly, until it coats the back of a spoon and reaches approximately 170°F. Test it by drawing your finger across the back of the spoon: if your finger leaves a trail in the custard, the custard has cooked to the right point. Immediately strain into a bowl and chill.

To make the cakes, preheat the oven to 400°F. Butter and flour 6 ramekins, 5 to 6 ounces each.

In the top of a double boiler over medium heat, heat the chocolate, butter, and Cognac, stirring until smooth and the chocolate and butter are melted. Set aside.

In a bowl, beat the granulated sugar and the 4 egg yolks until ribboned and light colored, 1 to 2 minutes. In another bowl, beat the 4 egg whites until stiff. Gently fold the egg whites into the egg yolk mixture. Sift the flour over the top and fold the flour and chocolate mixture into the egg mixture. Evenly distribute the mixture among the prepared ramekins. Place the ramekins on a baking sheet and bake until the cakes have risen and the tops just begin to crack, 10 to 12 minutes.

Immediately remove the ramekins from the oven and run a knife around the edges of the ramekins. Gently invert the ramekins onto 6 dessert plates. Spoon the custard sauce around the edges and dust the tops with confectioners' sugar. Garnish with raspberries and serve warm.

Serves 6

TO DRINK: Ruby port or late-harvest Zinfandel

apricot upside-down cake

If you enjoy comfort desserts, like our grandmothers used to make if we were very lucky, this cake is for you. The cake is moist and delicious, and the apricots that crown the top are sweet and flavorful.

1 cup (2 sticks) unsalted butter

$^3/_4$ cup firmly packed brown sugar

1 pound fresh apricots,
    halved and pitted

$2^1/_4$ cups all-purpose flour

1 tablespoon baking powder

$^1/_4$ teaspoon salt

$1^1/_2$ cups granulated sugar

3 large eggs, separated

$1^1/_4$ teaspoons vanilla extract

$^3/_4$ cup whole milk

Pinch of cream of tartar

1 cup heavy cream, for topping

1 tablespoon confectioners' sugar,
    for topping

Butter a 9-inch cake pan. Place the pan over medium heat and melt $^1/_4$ cup of the butter and the brown sugar in the bottom of the pan. Place the apricot halves on top of the melted butter and brown sugar, skin side down.

Preheat the oven to 350°F.

Sift together the flour, baking powder, and salt. Cream together the remaining $^3/_4$ cup butter and the granulated sugar in a bowl until light, 1 to 2 minutes. Add the egg yolks, 1 at a time, beating well after each addition. Add 1 teaspoon of the vanilla and mix well. Add the milk and the flour mixture alternately to the batter, folding well after each addition. Beat the egg whites to form soft peaks. Add the cream of tartar and continue to beat until stiff peaks form. Fold the whites into the cake batter. Spread the batter over the apricots and bake until a skewer inserted into the center comes out clean, 60 to 75 minutes.

Cool the cake for 10 to 15 minutes and run a knife around the edges of the pan to loosen it. Turn the cake over onto a serving platter and let it sit another 5 minutes. Remove the pan.

To serve, whip the heavy cream until soft peaks form. Sift the confectioners' sugar over the cream, add the remaining $^1/_4$ teaspoon vanilla, and fold together. Serve with the cake.

Serves 8 to 10

TO DRINK: Sauternes

cornmeal cake with cinnamon-poached pears

This is the moistest cornmeal cake you can imagine. Top it with warm cinnamon-poached pears for a favorite harvest or winter dessert. If possible, warm the pears in their syrup just before serving. A dollop of softly whipped cream sweetened with confectioners' sugar and flavored with vanilla extract will only make the dish even more delicious, if that's possible.

PEARS

2 cups port

2 cups water

6 cinnamon sticks

12 whole cloves, tied together
in cheesecloth

1 cup granulated sugar

6 medium-size Bosc pears, peeled,
quartered, and cored

CAKE

1 quart whole milk

$1/2$ cup plus 1 tablespoon granulated sugar

1 cup fine cornmeal

1 large egg

4 large egg yolks

$1/4$ cup ($1/2$ stick) unsalted butter,
at room temperature

Grated zest of 1 large orange

Confectioners' sugar, for dusting

To make the pears, in a saucepan over medium heat, bring the port and water to a boil, and add the cinnamon sticks, cloves, and granulated sugar. Add the pears and simmer until they are tender and can be easily pierced with a fork, 20 to 30 minutes. Discard the cloves and remove the pears and cinnamon sticks to a plate. Continue cooking the poaching liquid until reduced by half, 10 to 15 minutes. Reserve.

To make the cake, place the milk and granulated sugar in a saucepan over medium-high heat and bring to a boil. Gradually add the cornmeal, whisking constantly. Simmer until it is very thick, about 25 minutes. Let cool to lukewarm. Stir in the whole egg, egg yolks, butter, and orange zest.

Preheat the oven to 375°F. Butter a 9-inch cake pan.

Spread the cake batter in the prepared pan and bake until it just begins to turn golden and is firm to the touch in the center, 30 to 35 minutes. Turn out onto a cooling rack and let cool for 15 minutes.

To serve, cut the cake into wedges and place on individual plates. Spoon some pears, cinnamon sticks, and reduced poaching liquid around each piece of cake. Dust with the confectioners' sugar, and serve.

Serves 8

TO DRINK: Orange Muscat or late-harvest Pinot Gris

cool mint chocolate cookies

If you love the taste of chocolate and mint together, these cookies are sure to become the bane of your existence because you'll want to eat them by the dozens. They are deeply chocolaty, but not too sweet, with just the perfect hit of refreshing mint. Keep some of this dough in the freezer so you can slice and bake just what you need.

4 ounces bittersweet chocolate

12 ounces semisweet chocolate

$^{1}/_{4}$ cup ($^{1}/_{2}$ stick) unsalted butter

$^{3}/_{4}$ cup all-purpose flour

$^{1}/_{2}$ teaspoon baking powder

$^{1}/_{4}$ teaspoon salt

4 large eggs

1 cup sugar

1 tablespoon pure mint extract

12 ounces mini semisweet chocolate chips

$^{1}/_{2}$ cup chopped walnuts, toasted (page 7)

Melt the bittersweet chocolate, semisweet chocolate, and butter together in a double boiler over medium heat. Let cool for 10 minutes. In a bowl, combine the flour, baking powder, and salt.

In a bowl, beat the eggs with the sugar until they form a stiff ribbon, about 2 minutes. Add the melted chocolate mixture to the eggs. Sift the flour mixture on top and fold into the egg mixture along with the mint extract, mini chocolate chips, and walnuts. Cover with plastic wrap, place the dough in the refrigerator, and chill for 2 hours. When the dough is firm, remove from the refrigerator and divide into 4 logs, each 1$^{1}/_{2}$ inches in diameter and 6 to 8 inches long. Wrap each log in plastic wrap and refrigerate until cold and firm.

Preheat the oven to 350°F.

Slice the dough into $^{1}/_{4}$-inch slices and bake on an oiled or parchment-lined baking sheet until soft to the touch in the center, but slightly firm on the edges, 7 to 9 minutes. Remove from the baking sheets immediately and cool on racks.

Makes 5 dozen cookies

TO DRINK: Ruby port

coffee-hazelnut biscotti

Biscotti is Italian for "twice cooked." That's because you bake the dough in a loaf shape first, then slice the loaf into long cookies and bake them again. These joyfully crunchy morsels, their flavor deepened with coffee and studded with hazelnuts, are perfect for dunking into a caffè latte or for serving with a bowl of homemade vanilla bean ice cream. Make lots of these because they keep for weeks in an airtight container, they travel well, and everyone loves them.

1 cup hazelnuts

1 cup whole coffee beans, preferably
    French or Italian roast

$^1/_3$ cup heavy cream

1 cup plus 3 tablespoons sugar

$^1/_2$ cup (1 stick) unsalted butter

2 large eggs plus 1 large egg yolk

1 tablespoon coffee liqueur, preferably
    Tía Maria or Kahlúa

1 tablespoon plus 1 teaspoon instant coffee
    powder, dissolved in 1 tablespoon
    hot water

3 cups all-purpose flour

1 tablespoon cocoa powder

1 teaspoon baking powder

$^1/_2$ teaspoon baking soda

$^1/_4$ teaspoon salt

Preheat the oven to 350°F.

Place the hazelnuts on a baking sheet and bake until golden brown and fragrant, 10 to 12 minutes. Allow them to cool for 2 minutes and then rub them briskly in a kitchen towel to remove as much of the skin as possible. Chop the hazelnuts into $^1/_4$-inch pieces and set aside.

To make a glaze, bring the coffee beans, cream, and 3 tablespoons of the sugar to a boil in a small saucepan over medium-high heat. Remove from the heat and let steep for 1 hour.

Cream together the butter and remaining 1 cup sugar until light and fluffy. Add the eggs and egg yolk, 1 at a time, beating well after each addition. Add the coffee liqueur and instant coffee mixture. Sift together the flour, cocoa powder, baking powder, baking soda, and salt. Add the flour mixture in thirds, folding in the last third by hand with the hazelnuts. Chill the dough for 1 hour.

Divide the dough into 2 pieces and roll each into a 3 by 10-inch log. Flatten each slightly. Place on a baking sheet lined with parchment paper. Strain the coffee beans from the cream and discard the beans. Brush the tops of the dough logs with the glaze and bake until a skewer inserted into the center comes out clean, about 30 minutes. After the biscotti have been taken from the oven, brush them again with the glaze. While the biscotti are warm, slice them diagonally into $^1/_2$-inch slices.

Decrease the heat to 300°F. Place the biscotti on a baking sheet, cut side down, and bake for about 10 minutes. Turn the biscotti and continue to bake until dry, 10 minutes more.

Makes 3 dozen cookies

TO DRINK: Vin Santo or Amarone

pucker-up citrus crisps

If you love all things lemon as I do, you'll come back to this versatile cookie time and again. You will certainly see why I call these crisps "pucker up." Serve them as part of a "lemon trifecta" along with raspberry lemonade and creamy lemon sorbet presented in a scooped-out lemon. Your guests will be talking about this one for weeks!

1 cup sugar

1/4 cup lemon juice

1/4 cup (1/2 stick) unsalted butter, at room temperature

2 tablespoons heavy cream

1/2 teaspoon lemon oil

1 tablespoon grated lemon zest

1/2 teaspoon baking soda

1 cup cake flour

1 cup whole almonds, with skins, toasted and ground (page 7)

In a small saucepan, dissolve 1/4 cup of the sugar in the lemon juice over medium heat. Simmer until it thickens slightly, about 1 minute. Add the butter, stirring just until melted. Remove from the heat and transfer the mixture to a bowl. Add the cream, lemon oil, remaining 3/4 cup sugar, lemon zest, baking soda, flour, and almonds, and mix well. Refrigerate for 1 hour, until well chilled.

Preheat the oven to 350°F.

On a lightly floured surface, roll out the dough 1/8 inch thick. Cut into 1 1/2-inch-wide strips. Cut additional 1 1/2-inch–wide strips on the diagonal in the opposite direction, to make diamond shapes. Transfer the crisps to a baking sheet lined with parchment paper and bake until lightly golden on the edges, 8 to 10 minutes. While baking, the crisps will puff and crack slightly. Remove from the pan and cool on a rack before serving. When they are cool, they will be crisp.

Makes 3 to 4 dozen cookies

TO DRINK: Moscato

coffee-honey brûlée

If you've ever described yourself as being "busy as a bee," you were exaggerating. Did you know that honeybees tap two million flowers to make one pound of honey? That's a lot of work, but this elegant make-ahead dessert made with honey requires very little effort. Fragrant honey and smooth coffee-flavored custard is topped with a crunchy caramelized sugar shell that begs to be shattered. Who wouldn't love that? The baked brûlées can be stored for up to two days tightly covered with plastic wrap in the refrigerator, while the crispy shell can be made in a few minutes just before serving.

$1^1/_2$ cups heavy cream

2 cups whole milk

$^3/_4$ cup Italian or French roast
    coffee beans, coarsely cracked

9 large egg yolks

$^3/_4$ cup honey

1 teaspoon vanilla extract

$^1/_4$ cup super-fine sugar

In a saucepan over medium heat, warm the cream, milk, and coffee beans. Remove from the heat and let sit for 2 hours.

Preheat the oven to 325°F.

Strain the cream and milk through a fine mesh strainer lined with cheesecloth or a paper towel. Discard the coffee beans. In a bowl, whisk together the cream mixture and the egg yolks until blended. Whisk in the honey and vanilla. Divide the mixture evenly among 6 custard cups or ramekins, about 5 to 6 ounces each. Place the custard cups in a baking pan and fill the pan with enough boiling water to reach halfway up the sides of the cups. Bake until a knife or skewer inserted into the center of the custard comes out clean, 45 to 55 minutes. Remove the cups from the baking pan and cool on racks for at least 1 hour.

Preheat the broiler to high. Before serving, sprinkle the sugar evenly over the tops of the custards. Place on a baking sheet and set them 2 to 3 inches from the broiler. Broil until the sugar melts and caramelizes, 1 to 2 minutes. Serve at room temperature.

Serves 6

TO DRINK: Vin Santo

panna cotta with stewed grapes

Italian for "cooked cream," *panna cotta* sounds fancy but it's really very easy. The custard is smooth and creamy and the stewed grapes add a dash of color and sweetness. Use green or red grapes, whichever are sweetest. If you have muscat grapes, all the better. Garnish with a few grape halves and a sprig of mint. This is the quintessential autumn dessert that really pays homage to the noble grape.

CUSTARD

2 tablespoons cold water

1^3/$_4$ teaspoons granulated
    unflavored gelatin

1^1/$_2$ cups heavy cream

^{1}/$_2$ cup milk

^{1}/$_4$ cup sugar

Pinch of salt

SAUCE

1 pound sweet harvest grapes, plus
    some halved grapes, for garnish

^{1}/$_4$ cup sugar, or more, if needed

Sprigs of mint, for garnish

To make the custard, place the water in a small bowl. Sprinkle the gelatin over the water and set aside until the gelatin is softened, 5 minutes. Place the cream, milk, sugar, and salt in a saucepan. Bring to a boil over high heat, decrease the heat to medium, and boil for 1 minute, stirring constantly. Watch closely so it doesn't boil over. Remove from the heat and whisk in the gelatin mixture until dissolved. Pour into six 5-ounce ramekins and chill in the refrigerator for 3 hours.

In the meantime, to make the sauce, place the grapes and sugar in a saucepan over medium heat. Simmer until the grapes fall apart, 40 minutes. Pass the grapes and their liquid through a food mill and strain out the seeds and skin. Taste and add more sugar if needed. If you do add additional sugar, make sure that you stir until the sugar is dissolved. If the sauce is too thin, reduce further until it begins to thicken and coat the back of a spoon.

Just before serving, run a small knife around the edges of the ramekins. Dip the molds in boiling water just until loosened. Turn out onto serving plates and spoon the sauce around the edges. Garnish with the halved grapes and mint.

Serves 6

TO DRINK: Moscato

pineapple sorbet with extra-virgin olive oil and fleur de sel

When my Spanish friends put a platter of pineapple on the table for dessert, I thought, "Oh, how refreshing!" When they drizzled it with extra-virgin olive oil and sprinkled it with fleur de sel, I thought, "How bizarre!" But it really works. So I took the combination and made it into a sorbet. The acidity of the tangy pineapple is tempered by the rich, velvety olive oil and the counterpoint of the coarse salt. There's something about this combination that once you start, you just can't stop eating it!

1 ripe pineapple, peeled, cored, and cut into chunks

1 cup sugar, or more, if needed

6 tablespoons extra-virgin olive oil, for drizzling

Fleur de sel, for sprinkling

Place the pineapple chunks in a blender and puree until smooth. Strain through a fine mesh strainer into a clean bowl. Measure the puree. For each 4 cups of fruit puree, measure 1 cup sugar. Place approximately one-quarter of the fruit puree in a saucepan over medium heat. Add the correct amount of sugar and stir until the mixture simmers and the sugar is melted. Add this heated mixture back into the remaining fruit puree and stir together. Place in the refrigerator and chill until cold.

When the mixture is cold, freeze according to the instructions for your ice cream maker.

To serve, scoop the sorbet into bowls and drizzle a tablespoon of olive oil onto the top of each bowl of sorbet. Sprinkle with the fleur de sel and serve immediately.

Makes about 1 quart sorbet, to serve 6 to 8

TO DRINK: Late-harvest Semillon or Champagne

raspberry and zinfandel sherbet with warm berry compote

Imagine a blazing hot day in the middle of summer. Somebody hands you a beautiful, frosted martini glass filled with icy cold Zinfandel-raspberry sherbet peeking out from under a blanket of homemade berry compote. Refreshing, to say the least, and there's nothing I'd rather eat after a big lunch or dinner.

SHERBET

3 cups fruity Zinfandel

1 cup plus 2 tablespoons sugar

$1/3$ cup water

6 cups raspberries

COMPOTE

2 cups raspberries

$1/2$ cup water

$1/3$ cup sugar

1 piece of lemon peel, 2 inches long,
    removed with a vegetable peeler

$3/4$ cup blueberries

$3/4$ cup fraises des bois or wild
    strawberries (optional)

1 tablespoon crème de cassis

To make the sherbet, bring the Zinfandel, sugar, and water to a boil over high heat. As soon as it comes to a boil, pour it over the 6 cups raspberries. Let steep for 30 minutes.

In the meantime, to make the compote, puree 1 cup of the raspberries in a food processor or blender to obtain a smooth puree. Strain through a fine mesh strainer into a clean bowl and reserve. Place the water, sugar, and lemon peel in a medium-size pan over medium-high heat and bring to a boil. Decrease the heat to medium and add the blueberries. Cook until the blueberries just begin to crack, about 1 minute. Add the fraises des bois. Remove the lemon peel and discard. Stir in the raspberry puree, crème de cassis, and remaining 1 cup raspberries. You should have 2 cups of compote.

Finish the sherbet by pureeing the raspberry-Zinfandel mixture in a blender and straining through a fine mesh strainer. Refrigerate the mixture until well chilled. Freeze according to the instructions for your ice cream maker.

To serve, place the compote in a saucepan over medium heat and warm for about 1 minute. Scoop the sherbet into bowls and spoon the warm compote over the top. Serve immediately.

Makes about 1 generous quart sherbet, to serve 6

TO DRINK: Champagne or sparkling wine

tangerine ice cream with a citrus compote

Ice cream doesn't have to just be a summer treat. Try making this one in the winter with all the fresh citrus that's so readily available. Tangy tangerine ice cream topped with a warm compote of plumped raisins, blood oranges, passion fruit, kiwi, strawberries, and kumquats not only looks amazing but also tastes absolutely delicious.

ICE CREAM

7 tangerines

2 cups whole milk

2 cups heavy cream

$3/4$ cup sugar

8 large egg yolks

3 tablespoons freshly squeezed tangerine juice (from above tangerines)

2 tablespoons Grand Marnier

$1/4$ teaspoon vanilla extract

COMPOTE

$1^1/4$ cups freshly squeezed tangerine juice (from above tangerines)

2 tablespoons honey

$1/4$ cup golden raisins

6 kumquats, thinly sliced and seeds removed

2 kiwifruit, peeled and coarsely diced, for garnish

3 blood oranges, peeled and sectioned, for garnish (optional)

2 passion fruit, seeds only, for garnish (optional)

6 strawberries, sliced, for garnish

To make the ice cream, finely zest the peel of 2 tangerines and reserve. Remove the peel from the remaining 5 tangerines with a vegetable peeler and reserve. Squeeze all of the tangerines to yield a scant $1^1/2$ cups tangerine juice. In a large saucepan, combine the milk, heavy cream, sugar, and the tangerine peel and stir well. Scald over medium heat and turn off the heat. Let stand for 2 hours. Remove the tangerine peel and reserve.

In another saucepan, whisk the egg yolks for 5 seconds to break them up. Scald the cream mixture again. Add the cream mixture to the yolks, drop by drop, whisking constantly. Turn on the heat to medium. Stirring constantly, bring the mixture to 170°F, or just until it begins to thicken and coats the back of a wooden spoon. Whisk for 30 seconds to cool the mixture, and then strain immediately into a bowl. Add the reserved tangerine zest and the 3 tablespoons tangerine juice, the Grand Marnier, and vanilla extract. Refrigerate the mixture, tightly covered, until well chilled. Freeze according to the instructions for your ice cream maker.

To make the compote, combine the remaining $1^1/4$ cups tangerine juice, honey, raisins, and kumquats in a saucepan over medium-high heat and stir well. Heat the mixture just until it boils and cook for about 30 seconds. Let cool.

To serve, scoop the ice cream into bowls. Spoon the compote over the ice cream and garnish with the kiwifruit, blood oranges, passion fruit seeds, and sliced strawberries, distributing evenly. Serve immediately.

Makes about $1^1/2$ quarts ice cream, to serve 8

TO DRINK: Prosecco

lavender and toasted almond ice cream with warm baked figs

The scent of lavender always reminds me of my first trip to the south of France, when I scurried around the market buying Provençal lavender sachets and handmade lavender soaps to bring home to all of my friends. I still love the scent and find it wonedrfully calming. I either pick my own lavender flowers to dry in the sun or buy dried lavender at the health food store. (Make sure you don't buy lavender that's been sprayed with chemicals.) Imagine an ice cream made with lavender honey, lavender-caramel dust, and toasted almonds, an inspiration from the sunny south of France. *C'est si bon!*

LAVENDER-CARAMEL POWDER

5 tablespoons sugar

2 tablespoons dried lavender flowers

1 tablespoon water

ICE CREAM

2 cups whole milk

2 cups heavy cream

$^1/_2$ cup plus 2 tablespoons honey,
    preferably lavender honey

8 large egg yolks

$^3/_4$ cup almonds, toasted and chopped
    (page 7)

15 ripe figs

2 tablespoons port

To make the lavender-caramel powder, in a small, heavy saucepan over medium-high heat, combine the sugar, lavender, and water. Cook until the sugar dissolves and the mixture caramelizes, 2 to 3 minutes. Place on an oiled baking sheet and let cool. Grind in a spice grinder or clean coffee grinder to form a fine dust. Remove any large pieces and reserve. This can be made in advance and stored in an airtight container for up to a month.

To make the ice cream, in a large saucepan, scald the milk, heavy cream, and $^1/_2$ cup of the honey over medium heat. In another saucepan, whisk together the egg yolks. After the milk mix-ture has scalded, add it to the yolks, drop by drop at first and tablespoon by tablespoon after a minute, whisking constantly. When all of the milk mixture has been added to the yolks, add the reserved lavender powder and stir well. Place the pan over low heat and stir constantly until the mixture lightly coats the back of a wooden spoon and the temperature is 170°F. Remove from the heat immediately and strain into a bowl. Whisk for 30 seconds to cool. Chill for several hours in the refrigerator.

Freeze the ice cream according to the instruc-tions for your ice cream maker. During the last 2 minutes, add the chopped almonds and mix thoroughly.

Preheat the oven to 350°F. Drizzle a 13 by 9-inch baking dish with the remaining 2 table-spoons honey.

Halve the figs. Place the figs, cut side down, in a baking dish and bake until the figs are tender, about 20 minutes. Turn the figs, add the port, and baste with the liquid in the pan. Return the figs to the oven for 5 minutes more.

To serve, scoop the ice cream into bowls and top with the warm figs and their sauce.

Makes about 1 quart ice cream, to serve 10

TO DRINK: Demi-sec Champagne

espresso truffle ice cream

As a kid, I always loved chocolate-chip ice cream because I felt I was getting some secret extra bonus of real chocolate. When I came across the idea of folding tiny chocolate truffles into ice cream, I had to try it for nostalgia's sake. Well it's more spectacular than I remembered. Just as the espresso ice cream melts in your mouth, so do the rich chocolate truffles, creating that classic symphony of coffee and chocolate. I can't wait to stir chocolate truffles into mint, vanilla, raspberry, caramel, and chocolate ice creams.

1 cup espresso-roast coffee beans,
    coarsely cracked

2 cups whole milk

2$^1/_2$ cups heavy cream

$^3/_4$ cup sugar

9 large egg yolks

3 tablespoons coffee liqueur,
    such as Kahlúa or Tía Maria

4 ounces bittersweet chocolate

1 ounce unsweetened chocolate

5 tablespoons unsalted butter

Place the coffee beans, milk, 2 cups of the heavy cream, and sugar in a large saucepan over medium heat. Stir until the sugar is dissolved. Remove from the heat and let steep for 1 hour. Strain the mixture through a fine mesh strainer lined with cheesecloth or paper towels.

In another saucepan, beat the egg yolks together. Reheat the cream to scalding over medium heat. Pour about one-quarter of the hot cream into the egg yolks, whisking constantly. Add the rest of the cream, a little at a time, whisking constantly. Place the pan over low heat, stirring constantly with a flat-bottomed wooden spoon, and cook the mixture until it thickens enough to coat the back of the spoon, no hotter than 170°F. Immediately strain the mixture through a fine mesh strainer into a bowl. Whisk for a minute to cool the mixture slightly. Add 2 tablespoons of the coffee liqueur and chill in the refrigerator until cold.

In the meantime, make the truffles. Melt the bittersweet and unsweetened chocolates, butter, and the remaining $^1/_2$ cup cream in a small saucepan over low heat or over hot water, stirring constantly. Add the remaining 1 tablespoon coffee liqueur. Pour into an 8-inch pie plate or soufflé dish. Chill in the refrigerator until cold. When the chocolate is cold but still malleable, shape small truffles by dipping a $^1/_2$-teaspoon measuring spoon or a small melon baller into hot water and quickly scooping a truffle. Lay the truffles on a baking sheet in a single layer, making sure that they do not touch one another. When you have shaped them all, chill them in the freezer until firm, about 1 hour.

Freeze the ice cream according to the instructions for your ice cream maker. Fold the chilled truffles into the ice cream during the last 2 minutes of churning.

Makes about 1$^1/_2$ quarts ice cream, to serve 8

TO DRINK: Young tawny port

gianduja semifreddo

One of my favorite wine countries in the world is the Piedmont region in northwestern Italy. I love the Barolos and Barbarescos from this area, but I also love gianduja, the silky smooth hazelnut-flavored chocolate made there. This recipe calls for layering semifreddo (half frozen) creamy layers with luscious gianduja. If you've ever wept at the sight of your empty Nutella jar, then do not miss this one.

$3/4$ cup whole hazelnuts

6 ounces bittersweet chocolate, grated

6 amaretto cookies, crumbled

5 large eggs, separated

1 cup sugar

2 cups heavy cream

Preheat the oven to 350°F.

Place the hazelnuts on a baking sheet and bake until the skins start to crack, 5 to 10 minutes. Remove from the oven, place in a rough terry cloth towel, and rub to remove the skins. If some skin remains, repeat, but it is fine if a little skin is left. Chop the hazelnuts until finely ground. Alternatively, they can be finely ground in a food processor, but be careful not to make them into hazelnut butter.

In a bowl, combine the hazelnuts, chocolate, and amaretto cookies.

Line a 9 by 5-inch loaf pan with plastic wrap.

Beat the egg yolks with $1/2$ cup of the sugar until the mixture is a stiff ribbon, about 2 minutes. In another bowl, beat the egg whites until soft peaks form. Add the remaining $1/2$ cup sugar and continue to whisk until stiff peaks form. Finally, beat the heavy cream in a third bowl until stiff peaks form. Gently fold the egg yolk mixture into the egg whites. Fold in the beaten heavy cream.

Spoon one-third of the egg-cream mixture into the prepared pan. Spread to distribute evenly. Distribute half of the hazelnut-chocolate mixture evenly over the egg-cream mixture. Repeat the layers, ending with the egg-cream mixture. Smooth the top with a spatula. Cover with plastic wrap and freeze for several hours or overnight.

To serve, invert the pan onto a platter. Remove the plastic wrap. Cut into thick slices and serve.

Serves 8

TO DRINK: Madeira

after-dinner lemon freeze

Sgroppino (sgrow-pee-no) is the somewhat-difficult-to-pronounce Italian name for this deliciously refreshing and ever so slightly boozy take on a lemon milk shake. I first tasted one years ago in Italy, sitting along the Mincio River outside of Verona. I was so happy when my waiter took a small piece of scratch paper and wrote the recipe for me. Now I make it all the time and serve it for dessert with cookies.

1 pint vanilla ice cream, preferably homemade, softened at room temperature for 20 minutes

7 tablespoons lemon juice

1/3 cup vodka

In a blender, mix the ice cream, lemon juice, and vodka until it is smooth and pourable, 30 to 60 seconds.

Pour into glasses and serve immediately.

Serves 6

lemon verbena elixir

Lemon verbena is an herb native to South America, but it grows like a weed in the California Wine Country. Its earthy lemon scent is perfect for making tea, sorbets, and this luscious elixir. Keep a bottle chilled in your freezer and serve it after dinner with cookies or biscuits.

3 cups packed lemon verbena leaves

2 bottles (750 ml each) 100-proof vodka

3 cups sugar

4 cups water

Place the lemon verbena leaves in a large jar with 1 bottle of the vodka. Cover and place in a dark place for 5 days.

After 5 days, bring the sugar and water to a boil in a saucepan. Simmer for 5 minutes. Let the sugar syrup cool completely, then add it to the jar along with the remaining 1 bottle of vodka. Mix well, cover, and place in a dark place for 5 days.

After 5 days, strain and store 1 bottle in the pantry and 1 bottle in the freezer for ready use. Serve directly from the freezer in chilled glasses.

Makes 3 generous quarts, about 4 bottles

limoncello

Limoncello is a digestif made in Italy along the Amalti coast and on the islands of Ischia and Capri. It is pronounced lee-man-chello, the last part like the musical instrument. It doesn't require much elbow grease, just a good bit of patience and some waiting time.

15 lemons
2 bottles (750 ml each) 100-proof vodka
3$^1/_4$ cups sugar
5 cups water

Peel the lemons with a vegetable peeler, avoiding the white pith. Place the lemon peels in a large glass jar with 1 bottle of the vodka. Cover and place in a dark place for 40 days.

After 40 days, bring the sugar and water to a boil. Simmer for 5 minutes. Let the sugar syrup cool completely, then add it to the jar with the remaining 1 bottle vodka. Mix well, cover, and place in a dark place for 40 days.

After 40 days, strain and store 1 bottle at a time in the freezer until ready to use. Serve directly from the freezer in chilled glasses.

Makes 3 generous quarts, about 4 bottles

Opposite: Three refreshing lemon drinks, clockwise from left: Limoncello (this page), After-Dinner Lemon Freeze (page 217, top), and Lemon Verbena Elixir (page 217, bottom).

Conversion Charts

VOLUME

Formulas:

1 teaspoon = 4.93 milliliters
1 tablespoon = 14.79 milliliters/3 teaspoons
1 cup = 236.59 milliliters/16 tablespoons
1 liter = 202.88 teaspoons/67.63 tablespoons/4.23 cups

U.S	Imperial	Metric
1 teaspoon	$1/6$ fl oz	5 ml
2 teaspoons	$1/3$ fl oz	10 ml
1 tablespoon (3 teaspoons)	$1/2$ fl oz	15 ml
2 tablespoons	1 fl oz	30 ml
$1/4$ cup	2 fl oz	60 ml
$1/3$ cup	3 fl oz	90 ml
$1/2$ cup	4 fl oz	120 ml
$2/3$ cup	5 fl oz ($1/4$ pint)	150 ml
$3/4$ cup	6 fl oz	180 ml
1 cup	8 fl oz ($1/3$ pint)	240 ml
$1^1/4$ cups	10 fl oz ($1/2$ pint)	300 ml
2 cups (1 pint)	16 fl oz ($2/3$ pint)	480 ml
$2^1/2$ cups	20 fl oz (1 pint)	600 ml
1 quart	32 fl oz ($1^2/3$ pint)	1 l

WEIGHT

Formulas:

1 ounce = 28.35 grams
1 pound = 453.59 grams/16 ounces
1 kilogram = 2.2 pounds

U.S./Imperial	Metric
$1/2$ oz	15 g
1 oz	30 g
2 oz	60 g
$1/4$ lb	115 g
$1/3$ lb	150 g
$1/2$ lb	225 g
$3/4$ lb	350 g
1 lb	450 g

LENGTH

Formulas:
1 inch = 2.54 cm
1 foot = .3 m/12 inches
1 cm = .39 inch
1 m = 3.28 feet/39.37 inches

Inch	Metric
$^1/_4$ inch	6 mm
$^1/_2$ inch	1.25 cm
$^3/_4$ inch	2 cm
1 inch	2.5 cm
6 inches ($^1/_2$ foot)	15 cm
12 inches (1 foot)	30 cm

TEMPERATURE

Formulas:
$^9/_5$ C + 32 = F
(F – 32) x $^5/_9$ = C

Fahrenheit	Celsius/Gas Mark
250°F	120°C/gas mark $^1/_2$
275°F	135°C/gas mark 1
300°F	150°C/gas mark 2
325°F	160°C/gas mark 3
350°F	180 or 175°C/gas mark 4
375°F	190°C/gas mark 5
400°F	200°C/gas mark 6
425°F	220°C/gas mark 7
450°F	230°C/gas mark 8
475°F	245°C/gas mark 9
500°F	260°C

Index